Make Mine A Mule

Some folks need a *high* horse
For their self-esteem is low.
Others need a heavy horse
And don't worry if it's slow.
Some must have a winner
For them nothing else will do
But a flash little nag
That will always win the *Blue*.
Others must have colour
To add brightness to their day;
Golden Palomino
Or nursery dappled grey.
Some folk think that common
And would be ashamed to own
Aught but black, brown or bay,
A good horse of sober tone.
When it comes to equines
Only one can fill my book
That's the long-eared bastard
With the strangely donkey look.
Any shape or colour,
But he never is a fool.
I look for brains and sense,
Which is why I chose a mule.

Ann Walker

Chapter One

When my hostess put down her coffee cup and fixed me with a stern stare across the lunch table, I felt a tremor of apprehension. I had driven for two hours to collect the four-year-old mule she had offered me, and on arrival had been hustled past the animal tethered in the grassy lane outside the charming cottage, with the information that lunch was ready. Over the meal, which was not only ready but also exceptionally good, the conversation roamed over many subjects but barely touched on the reason I was here. However good food and interesting conversation were a soothing combination, and it was only when my charming hostess began to speak that I felt any real anxiety.

'Certain conditions must be met before I agree to the sale.' Her voice, I felt, had taken on a steely touch.

I carefully replaced my own fine china cup in its saucer and met her eyes.

'Yes?' I murmured. It was a question—not agreement.

'First you must swear on all you hold sacred, that you will never, ever sell her to anyone else without telling me and giving me the chance to buy her back.'

I happily agreed to that. After all, it was to

my advantage; if I found I didn't like or want her, I could simply return her.

'You must be absolutely sure you truly like her.'

Well—what I had seen of her I felt quite confident on that one, but as I nodded and opened my mouth she continued in a firm voice, fixing me with a steely eye.

'And Pepita must like you.'

'You mean . . .' I floundered. 'We must like each other?'

'Exactly—it has to be mutual.'

'But—how will we know?'

'I shall know.' Firm emphasis on the pronoun.

'I see,' I murmured, but I didn't really see—not then at any rate. Understanding came much later. By now I was beginning to seriously doubt the success of my two-hour journey. I had bought many horses over the years, and I alone had always been the one who must like or not like to clinch the deal. I was prepared to go out and submit to the test, but there was more to come.

'If we cannot load her into the float on our own without any force or trauma, I cannot let you have her.' She paused, her expression as uncompromising as her words. I knew she meant it. This then, I thought, was it. The lunch and the conversation had both been very enjoyable but I had not driven for two hours with a horse float behind me, something I

2

MAKE MINE A MULE

The Story of a Friendship

Ann Walker

CHIVERS

British Library Cataloguing in Publication Data available

This Large Print edition published by AudioGO Ltd, Bath, 2013.
Published by arrangement with the Author

U.K. Hardcover   ISBN 978 1 4713 3536 5
U.K. Softcover   ISBN 978 1 4713 3537 2

Printed and bound in Great Britain by
TJ International Limited

PREFACE

I have always felt convinced that survival of death and the existence of a soul was not confined to humans. Over the years I had seen so much nobility and beauty of spirit in the animals I was privileged to know that I felt sure that Heaven, or whatever life existed after this present one, was not reserved exclusively for human kind. I feel with those who declare that if there is no place in Heaven for the animals they have known and loved in this life then they would prefer to go elsewhere.

Pepita was one of the most truly beautiful souls I ever knew, and twenty-eight years is surely long enough to know another living being. I still miss her and think of her every day of my life. This book is a tribute to her, with hope that somewhere, someone reading it will look at their own much-loved equine companion and feel comforted by the belief that life, in some form or other, continues . . .

disliked at the best of times, just to drive back again.

Pepita was four years old, only trained to lead and tether. As mules went, she was small, but like all her kind had the combined strength of a horse and a donkey. The common saying, *Stubborn as a mule* settled in my mind, and every unwilling donkey or horse I had ever helped load flashed through it, with the strong male arms helping them up the ramp. We had none of those handy; there was only us, two average women. This mule had never been in a horse float in her life. Why should she get in willingly now to leave the only home she had ever known, and this kind woman who obviously cared so much for her? Maybe I should just get in the car now and leave?

Lost in my gloomy thoughts I had not registered that my hostess had risen from the table and was reaching for something off the shelf behind her.

'These,' she held up an unopened packet of sweet biscuits, 'are her favourite—they might help.'

I had heard of bowls of oats, many helpers with strong arms, ropes, even cattle goads to persuade unwilling equines to walk up echoing wooden ramps into the dark cavern of strange horse floats that would take them they knew not where—but a packet of biscuits!

However, it was with a faint glimmer of hope I took up my stance behind Pepita as

3

instructed, agreeing with her owner that it was best if she led her up the ramp. With a running commentary of sweet talk to the mule, she pointed out the biscuits and offered one. Tentatively Pepita placed a hoof on the bottom of the ramp as she munched the treat.

Slowly, a step and a biscuit. All four feet were on the boards. Finally, as she took the last biscuit in the packet, she was in and I hoisted the ramp and quickly fastened it. We had done it—without fuss or trauma. I could not wait to set out on the long drive home. Longer than the journey here, time-wise anyway, for I, in my anxiety not to upset her in any way, drove so slowly and carefully that the two-hour journey took three, leaving me plenty of time to reflect how the events of five years ago had led to this moment—or had it really begun long before that when I saw my first mule and was entranced?

I did not guess that I was embarking on the longest relationship—twenty-eight years—I would ever share with an animal.

Chapter Two

On that long journey home I thought about the events that had led up to this moment. I did not have the radio on, as I wanted to be able to hear any untoward noises from my passenger, so I was left with nothing but my thoughts. They led me back to England and the Second World War and the moment when my fascination with mules first began.

My father, who farmed in the English Midlands, had agreed to take a much-needed holiday between the Hay harvest and the Grain harvest, so there we were in early June spending a week at Blackpool, the huge seaside resort on the North West Coast.

It should have been summer but bitter winds and rain from the North Sea drove us away from the beach and to indoor entertainment. Blackpool Tower, famous not only as a man-made landmark, but for its many diversions, housed the Tower Circus. There were two animal acts that I have never forgotten: one was a troupe of domestic cats who bounded into the ring with their woman handler without any restraints, and the other was a small mule, billed as *unrideable*. A neat little fellow, dark brown in colour and only about nine or ten hands high. He lived up to his reputation; no one could even get on him. He achieved this without violence or viciousness. Many years later I would see Pepita prevent people she didn't like do exactly the same thing and stop them mounting her without any danger to them or indeed any violence. I didn't know how she achieved it any more than I did the little mule in Blackpool.

Like the cats, he was quite unrestrained in the ring; part of the act he performed was to lie down on his side on an iron bedstead complete with bedding. Before relaxing with his head on the pillow he reached over his shoulder and pulled up the blanket with his teeth.

I was enchanted. I had my own pony at home who I loved dearly and was forever showing off her one trick, self taught (I could claim no credit), when given a carrot she would put it carefully on the ground, get the long end in her teeth, put a front hoof on the fat end and break it in half. It always impressed visitors, and she got a lot of carrots.

It was about three years before I met another mule. Mules were thin on the ground in England in those days, long before they became popular and a thriving society was formed. Our farm was a scattered one bisected by a rough bridle track known as Bent Lane. There was an even rougher offshoot of this that had grown almost impassable due to a fallen tree half way along. It lay between tall hazelnut hedges, had grassed over with time, and was not only off the beaten track but also an ideal camping ground for the gypsies who passed this way at least twice a year. These were genuine Romanies who drove colourful painted wagons pulled by horses, usually skewbald or piebald, and spoke the old Romany language. They always had one or two Lurcher dogs and a cage of three or four laying hens and a rooster swinging beneath one of the wagons. When they camped, these birds were let out to forage for themselves, and though quite free, never left the vicinity of the wagons, returning to base to roost in their hanging home at night. Gypsies were feared by the country people and disliked by the farmers who considered them thieving vagabonds, and tried to get the local police to move them on.

My father had different views; he *liked* the gypsies and never tried to speed them on their way. On the contrary, he often employed them for seasonal work such as potato picking. As the part of the Lidgetts lane where they liked to camp lay between two of our fields, it was generally assumed to be part of our farm, so if my father told the police he was happy to have them there they were not hassled, and if they stole they did it from our neighbours, not us. When they learned that my father was very fond of the hazelnuts that grew in such abundance in the unpruned hedges where they camped, they made a point of leaving a fair proportion of the harvest for him.

A friend of mine whose parents farmed the next farm was enraged when she looked out of her bedroom window and saw the old Gypsy grandmother walk across their field towards her thoroughbred mare and calmly remove its head collar. I was not sure when she told me this whether her fury was directed at the gypsy

7

or the horse, for the reason she was wearing a head collar was because she was normally hard to catch; yet she had allowed the old woman to walk straight up to her and remove it.

Like my father, I had no fear of the gypsies, and recognised the stories the country people told of Romanies stealing children and bringing them up as their own for the utter nonsense they were.

When I was about five years old I had a memorable experience. My father had taken me, as he often did, to walk round the farm with him. We were going through one of the fields alongside the Lidgetts and, as so often at this time of the year (Spring), a couple of vans were parked there. I was trailing behind my father who was walking head down engrossed in the soil and the new seedlings just beginning to break through. A little girl about my own age was standing at the fence. She beckoned me over. I watched my father's back moving away and hurried over to make friends. Mickey, our tiny little terrier, mirrored my action, noting that my father was not observing what he was doing, and deciding it was a more interesting option to follow me, he joined me at the fence.

The girl jerked her head, rampant with uncombed black curls in striking contrast to my short, neat and very straight blonde bob.

'Want to come in?' she asked.

I had never scrambled through a fence so

quickly. Mickey was ahead of me and already bounding up the steps of the nearest van. The woman standing on the top step smiled at me and indicated I should follow her inside. I was intrigued by the half door, like a stable door, which she closed behind us, and while the child pointed out to me all the interesting features of the interior of the van, her mother spread thick slices of bread with blackberry jam, including one for Mickey, which he appeared to enjoy as much as I did.

I was just licking the last of the jam from my sticky fingers when my father's smiling face appeared over the half door. He thanked the woman politely for looking after me, so I followed his example and thanked her for the bread and jam, and then we set off home. On the way he confessed that he had not noticed the absence of either Mickey or me until he had reached the other side of the field but had guessed where we were.

Apart from a cautionary, 'Maybe it would be better not to mention this to your mother,' nothing else was said.

I was conscious that I had been honoured and was pretty sure no one else in the district had been inside one of the colourful wagons. I never had another opportunity but I was always pleased to see the gypsies arrive and often stopped to talk to them when I rode past their camp on my pony.

It was about ten years later when I reined

in my spotted mare, Freckles, to exchange greetings with a man whittling away at a stick. He asked me where I had got my striking leopard-spotted pony, and when I told him she had come from a dealer who had bought her in Ireland, he nodded sagely and said she had probably been bred by Romanies.

I returned his interest in my mare by asking about the sleek bay pony of about thirteen hands tethered with the three coloured ponies favoured by the gypsies. Unlike its rather scrawny companions it looked in peak condition. I thought everything about it was beautiful—especially its rather large ears.

'Is that a mule?' I asked.

'He is that. Not many people know, they just think he is a very ugly pony with those great long ears.'

'He is not ugly,' I protested. 'He's beautiful. And I love his ears!'

'I don't know about that, but he is strong all right. He pulls a wagon all by himself—takes two of them ponies to pull the other one. I reckon he is as strong as your Dad's Shire horses.'

The next day I was in my bedroom gloomily packing my trunk for my return to boarding school when I heard the clip of hooves and the rumble of wheels. I ran to the window; the gypsies were moving on. The leading caravan was rolling at a smart pace with the mule in the shafts. The second van had two of the ponies abreast and the third hitched behind. I watched 'til they were out of sight.

Chapter Three

As I continued my drive home, my thoughts ran to the more recent events that had led to this moment. Many years had passed and I was now half a world away from the gypsy's mule I had thought so handsome. I was married now and had children of my own. My husband had grown up with ponies just as I had, and loved them as much. We also loved donkeys, and it had been a wrench parting with our ponies and our little donkey, Henry, when we emigrated to Australia.

We had been to a big Donkey Show before we left England and were impressed by what these tough and canny little equines could do. They were ridden, driven, competed in obstacle courses, and even jumped. We promised each other that when we were settled again we would breed donkeys.

Our first four years in Australia were spent in Tasmania. Here we settled on a hilly farm on the North West Coast ideal for breeding donkeys, only to come up against a big snag— there did not seem to be any donkeys available in Tasmania. I located two in a local zoo and another two in the Midlands that had been owned by the late Nan Chauncy, the well-known children's author. None were for sale however. The proprietor of the small private zoo absolutely refused to consider selling them, as they were too big an attraction, he told us. Nan Chauncy's husband said he could not consider parting with his, as Nan had loved them so much.

The frustration of this was further exacerbated by my small daughter, Ruth, barely three years old, who had been particularly fond of Henry and who continued to ask me sadly, 'Where is my Henry donkey? I *want* my Henry donkey.' She had been asking this since we left England and I had blithely promised to get her another donkey, never for one moment suspecting that we were heading for a place in the world where it seemed there were no donkeys available.

But a promise is a promise and I eventually imported six wild donkeys from Mainland Australia. I tried to import them through stock agents at first but they refused to take anyone wanting donkeys seriously. Then I saw a firm advertising that they could get any sort of pet, so I tried them. They deemed donkeys pets, so on a wet and stormy day, following an even stormier night on the Bass Strait, six young donkeys tottered out of a horse float into our paddock. These became the nucleus of the Keysoe Donkey Stud.

Judging by the reaction, the rest of the

people in Tasmania thought importing donkeys was a bizarre thing to do. They were featured in all the State's media, newspapers, Radio and TV. I was constantly giving interviews, talking about donkeys and writing about them. I, who in reality had little experience of them, became an expert overnight.

A constant stream of visitors came just to look at them. Among them was a mule lover, who told me about a mule he had known on a Victorian sheep station, and my desire for one was fired all over again.

I had not even seen another mule since the one in England. Getting to know and love my wild donkeys, and noting the subtle difference between them and ponies, made me even more intrigued by mules. I read everything I could lay my hands on about them. Most of this material originated in America where I learned mules were big—in every sense of the word.

Soon I felt I was an expert, although in truth all I had was a smattering of what an old country character in my childhood scornfully described as *book larnin*. I had no hands-on experience at all and had only ever see two mules in my life, and that was many years ago. Such was my confidence in my own knowledge that I wrote an article on mules, which was published in the prestigious *Hoofs & Horns* magazine here in Australia. I think my elevation to 'donkey expert' and the fact that I had written several pieces about donkeys for the equine press must have gone to my head. The upshot of this was a letter from a reader in Victoria—we were still in Tasmania at the time—telling me she had both ponies and donkeys, and asking my advice on breeding a mule.

I have no idea what advice I gave her from the depths of my ignorance but I had a charming note back thanking me for my helpful advice.

Unbeknownst to me, this was the beginning of Pepita.

Just over a year later I heard from the lady in Victoria again to tell me she had her mule foal, and she enclosed a small black and white snap.

The mother, she told me was a crossbred Exmoor mare she had chosen on my advice, for her excellent temperament. I remembered telling her to choose a mare of good temperament because the mother influenced the foal so much. This I had learned in my reading, not from experience. She added as a footnote that there would be no more mules, as the jack had met with a freak accident, and she did not intend to replace him.

I wrote a brief note back, congratulating her on her success and thanking her for the photo and heard no more 'til the letter offering me the mule, now four years old and called Pepita.

All this passed through my mind as I drove. I wondered too why I had been so excited at the prospect of actually owning this little mule, as by now, I had hands-on experience in the form of Juanita, a beautiful black mule who I bought as a five-month-old weanling from her breeder. I decided it must be because I felt responsible for her existence. Juanita would become famous in years to come when owned by Patsie Sinfield, the well-known Endurance Rider, when she became the first mule to complete the Quilty hundred mile endurance ride and the star of Patsie's book about her, *Juanita The Wonder Mule.*

As I drove I thought sentimentally that Juanita would be pleased to have another mule for company.

I was wrong.

From the moment Pepita stepped out of the float, looked round and brayed, presumably to announce her presence, they both made it clear they were not interested in being friends. Pepita had a truly shocking voice. The loudest foghorn blast I have ever heard. Totally different to Juanita, whose voice was more like a horse's whinny. I have since learned that mule's voices are quite individual; a huge range within the parameters of a horse's whinny and a donkey's bray.

The bray announcing her arrival brought everyone on the scene to see the creature that could make such a horrendous noise. Equine heads, both horse and donkey, peered over fences in astonishment, and Juanita looked shocked. I did not realise that mules do not actually know they are mules. They think of themselves as horses. The first creature they see in life is their mother, who is a horse, so naturally they think they are the same and always gravitate to horses rather than donkeys. Hinnys, who are the same cross the other way round—donkey mother and horse father— think they are donkeys.

My family crowded round to look at her, and remarked that she was rather small. Juanita was fourteen hands, eight inches taller than Pepita, who was only twelve hands.

'Just right for you children,' I told them blithely. 'We'll have her trained in no time. She won't be much trouble; she has been well handled all her life and has already been taught to lead and tether.'

In the weeks and months that followed, I would have cause to eat my words, many times. What I said was true, but it was also *all* she had learned—apart from a taste for sweet biscuits. She had also, it seemed, picked up a few hang-ups along the way.

One thing that never crossed my mind was taking up her previous owner's offer to return her.

Chapter Four

My father had been very fond of saying, 'A little knowledge is a dangerous thing.' Never had I realised the truth of this as clearly as when I began to train Pepita.

My first six wild donkeys were all young and untouched; I started with a clean slate. The same applied to their progeny. I did not follow any guidance but my own intuition. An intuition, which deserted me with Pepita, to be replaced by a sublime overconfidence. With the donkeys I concentrated first on winning their trust. I spent up to three weeks with each one in a yard just leaning on the fence and talking to them 'til they would come up to me for titbits, then I stroked them and talked some more, finally slipping a halter on them. Then I groomed them and finally put saddles and bridles on them and taught them the basics of good equine manners. This *steady as she goes method* paid off. They were soon safe and reliable for my young children to ride, and we were even asked to take them to fundraising events to give rides to children. I was happy to do this, and trusted them implicitly, because I was eager to show people how splendid donkeys were.

I embarked on Pepita's education using the same method. The only difference was she was not wild and untouched. She was also older. Had I really thought, it just might have occurred to me than it was reasonable to assume that at four years old someone had tried to teach her something. I did not ask, and no information was offered. I knew that someone trained the young ponies that were bred on the property so I should have made inquiries, not assumed that she was untouched like my young donkeys.

Instead, I persuaded myself I could actually skip much of the early steps and get stuck straight in with her serious education. Mistake number one. She was prepared to give me limited trust because I was a woman and her previous owner had always treated her kindly. I do not think I was lied to, except perhaps by omission, but in later conversations it was let slip that the person who trained her breeder's young ponies had attempted something with her, I think probably training to harness, with such disastrous results he refused to do any more with her. She was dearly loved by her owner who felt that she herself was too old take the job on, but wanted to see her living a useful and happy life—hence her letter offering her to me. I wish I had known this at the time, it would not have deterred me from having her, but given me a greater understanding, and I would have been sensible of the trust being placed in me.

She had never been off the quiet rural

property where she was born. She knew absolutely nothing of the world and its terrors, such as traffic. She been taught to lead but had never been led anywhere. She had also been taught to tether, and it seemed she had spent most of her time on the tether. In a subsequent conversation with her former owner, I was told that this was so, the explanation being that if running in a paddock she was either bullied by the horses or bullied the donkeys. When later on I tentatively turned her out with other equines I found this totally untrue. Quite the contrary in fact. She made good friends with donkeys and formed very close relationships with ponies. She was quite happy in the company of either. But in those early days I took this information at face value and kept her in a yard.

I spent as many hours with her as I could, but because she was not technically wild, I did not spend nearly enough time gaining her confidence. I rushed through this stage; something one should never be tempted to do when training any animal. I soon had her wearing a saddle and bridle, both of which she accepted. With the wisdom of hindsight I should have noted the signs of stress. The large ears that moved continually, the huge eyes, grown even larger, the tenseness I could feel when I put my hand on her neck. After my success with the donkeys, I was so sure that I knew what I was doing that I didn't see them, or if I did, I ignored them.

Impressed with her acceptance of the saddle, I leaned across her back to accustom her to the sensation of weight. She stood still; too still, like a coiled spring. I should have stopped there, but no; impressed more with my own progress than hers, I swung my leg over and was astride her very briefly. I don't know exactly what she did but I hit the ground with such force I actually saw stars. I don't know why, because it was my butt not my head that I landed on, which subsequently developed the largest and most spectacular bruise I ever had. I could not sit comfortably for weeks, and for several days could hardly walk.

Pepita stood in a corner of the yard, her expressive eyes fixed on me, her nostrils dilated and tremors rippling through her whole frame. She stood quite still as I hobbled over to her and removed the saddle and bridle. I knew that she had not intended to hurt me; sheer fear and panic had controlled her actions. I spoke softly to her and took the gear off as quietly and gently as I could before hobbling into the house to think about what had happened. No doubt left alone in the yard she did the same. Looking back, I can see that this was a defining moment in our relationship, albeit a painful one for me.

I ran myself a hot bath, remembering how my mother had always got us in the tub after childhood falls from ponies, and lay soaking and thinking. I knew it was entirely my own fault because I was so anxious to see her being ridden, and she had seemed so accepting of the things I put on her, I had ignored the signs of her anxiety. I knew that by rushing things I had actually slowed them down. I would have to go right back to square one—and I wouldn't even be able to do that until my bruises subsided. However, there was nothing to stop me continuing to develop my relationship with her.

I spent a lot of time over the next few weeks talking to her, grooming her, and of course, giving her titbits. It was time well spent; over the twenty-eight years of our life together, that was the only time I came off her.

Chapter Five

'In the World of Mules there are no Rules,' wrote Ogden Nash. Like so many of his pithy comments, this is very true.

I had had ponies for most of my life and felt I knew what made them tick. Since the arrival of my six wild donkeys I had noted the subtle differences between them and ponies, often one of attitude as much as anything. I had also been lucky enough to buy Juanita when she was only five months old. She had been carefully handled from birth, and as a weanling, was more streetwise than Pepita at four years old, so comparing behaviour did not help me a great deal. In any case, individualism is as much part of a mule's make up as long ears.

Mules are genetically equally horse and donkey, and it has been said fairly truthfully, that a mule is a horse in the middle and a donkey at the extremities; they have a body like a horse but the ears and feet are those of a donkey. But these are mere physical qualities easy to see, they didn't help me to understand mule character, which I expected to be a neat blend of the two, in the same way as their physical appearance. It didn't seem to work like that; I learned to appreciate Ogden Nash's observation. At times they behave like horses, at others like donkeys, but more often that not they are quintessential mule, and that can vary greatly from one mule to another.

Over the years, as well as the reading material on mules I eagerly devoured, I had met people who had experience of them, and everything I heard had fed my desire to have a mule of my own. Shortly after I brought donkeys into Tasmania I had a visitor, one of the many who came to see them for their arrival, described by one reporter, as the animal story of the year, hit the headlines. He told me about a mule he had met on a mainland sheep station where he had worked.

'It was well into its thirties yet could still

work three shifts to every one the horses did. Everyone wanted to ride him because he was the same all day; you had to fight a too fresh horse in the morning and urge on a flagging one at night. What is more, his walk was the same speed as a mob of trotting sheep; he didn't have to keep breaking into a jog. A day on him was much less tiring than on a horse—however good,' he told me.

Many years later I was to discover the truth of this for myself. All I could do then was listen and read anything and everything on mules that I could lay hands on, and soon became such an expert that the prestigious glossy monthly *Hoofs & Horns* published the article I wrote on mules that would ultimately bring Pepita and me together in one of the closest, certainly the longest, relationship I ever had with any animal.

That was in the past and the future. Now, in the present, I had to earn Pepita's trust, and to do so it was necessary to curb my own impatience.

I went right back to the beginning and didn't attempt to put a saddle on her until I had done much more handling of her. I groomed her 'til her coat shone, combed her tail as well as her mane, and I walked round her with my hand on her rump. I did things on both sides of her and behind so that she got used to me close to her, and always I talked to her. I picked up her feet and cleaned them out. One of her dainty donkey-like hooves was worn down one side more than the other, evidence that she had walked in circles on her tether. There was also a small gap in her mane caused by the collar rubbing it. Things I had not noticed before. Her mane was unusual in that it was floppy. Most mules have stand-up manes like their donkey forbears. Over the years, I was to have many people telling me quite confidently that she was a hinny. 'You can always tell,' they said, 'because hinnies have floppy manes.' Well they couldn't always tell. I had seen Pepita's pony mother and a photo of her donkey father. She was a mule.

Before I even put the saddle on her again I left it over the railings of the yard where she could walk up to it, sniff it, nibble it if she wished, and satisfy herself it was harmless. I saddled her and unsaddled her umpteen times, took her for walks in it, lunged her and long reined her. In short, treated her more like a pony.

Lunging is getting a horse to run round you in large circles on a lead rope several times normal length. Instructions are given with a long whip, like a ringmasters, the horse is never, or should not be, hit with this. It is used to give messages: go faster, slow down, and stop. I did this with the saddle on in order for her to grow accustomed to it, staying there while she moved and things flapped. Long reining is training for the bit so that the horse understands that pressure on one side means turn that way, and on both sides at once means stop. I always gave her verbal commands at the same time.

She grew more relaxed and appeared to enjoy these training sessions. Now she had confidence in me she learned quickly. A horse show was coming up with, probably a first for Australia, a class for mules. As well as the led class where all she needed to do was look beautiful and behave reasonably well, there was a class for long reining. I decided that it would be a wonderful experience for her.

She behaved perfectly and was acquitting herself well in the long rein class, stopping, starting and turning as requested, and I was glowing with pride when the judge took the reins from me to try her for himself. Pepita did not see him do this, as of course she had her back to us. Off she went, away from me to the other side of the ring. I watched her, delighted how she had come on since the day we had both fallen from grace. She had put up much the best performance, and there was no doubt she would win the class, so I told myself as she did a perfect turn on the other side of the ring to make the return journey. She stopped dead when she saw me, then turned to look who was on the other end of the reins, then back to me on the other side of the ring. Her head went up, her large luminous eyes reflecting shock and horror when she saw that a strange man had replaced me. For a moment she stood quite still taking this in, then she opened her mouth.

'OHMYGOD!' her foghorn bellow really did seem to be saying that as it reverberated round the ground, making audience and competitors, both four legged and two, turn to see who or what could make such a noise. At the same time she responded to the instructions from behind her to move forward—at high speed! The judge had to run; she ignored any pressure on the reins to stop her, even his desperate, 'Whoa!' He handed the reins back to me with the terse, and breathless, comment that she needed a lot more training, and placed her at the bottom of the class.

I was mortified, and my husband did not improve matters by telling me it was very amusing. The three children agreed, grinning. We were half way home when it was pointed out to me that it was obvious she had no idea the judge had taken over 'til she turned and saw me at the far side of the ring and realised I was not in charge.

'You should be pleased; it showed you really had won her confidence,' my husband told me.

'Hmm.' I thought about this and knew he was right. The winning or losing of a blue ribbon could not compare with the miracle of knowing Pepita trusted me—at last.

'I thought she was pretty smart to realise what had happened and you were not on the other end of the reins,' one of the children sagely remarked.

I remembered a comment I had recently read in an American magazine:

Mules are said to be stupid when their intelligence exceeds that of their handler.

Yes,' I agreed, 'it was smart. But that's mules for you.'

Chapter Six

I am ashamed to admit that I was not game to be the one to ride Pepita first. After all, I reasoned, I had bought her as a mount for the children. I doubt if I fooled anyone, even myself. When I had done about everything possible to educate her except actually get on her back I looked at my children, who were looking at Pepita, somewhat sceptically I felt, and with a bright smile and an even brighter voice said, 'Right . . . who is going to get on her?'

With one voice they answered. Max said, 'Me,' and the other two said, 'Max.'

'Right, get your hard hat.'

He mounted while I stood by her head, murmuring sweet, and I hoped, soothing nothings into her long ears, which were moving

27

back and forth. But she stood still and her large and expressive eyes were calm I noted. I looked up at Max; he looked quite relaxed so I walked forward leading Pepita. She walked quietly at my side.

After we had been up and down the drive and round the yard a few times Max said, 'Stay there, I want to go by myself with her.'

I threw an anxious look at Pepita, which she didn't return, and told him to go ahead, adding, 'But keep it to a walk.'

He did, down the drive, but came back at a steady trot. Max was grinning cheerfully and Pepita's ears were pricked and they came to a stop at my side by mutual agreement. This was the beginning of a wonderful partnership between them and was probably the best thing to happen for her at the time to further her education. Max, although only eight years old, was an accomplished rider and was riding a Welsh Mountain pony stallion at Shows for his owner.

For the next couple of years Pepita claimed her donkey ancestry and went to Donkey Club taking part in Trail Rides and Games days and doing it so well that we decided to let her be a pony and go to pony club. She was accepted at Pony Club on condition she didn't upset the horses. Those who have never seen a donkey sometimes freak out and make utter fools of themselves when they first meet one of their long-eared cousins. But Pepita wasn't a donkey, she was a mule, half horse, and she never met a horse who saw her as anything but the same as themselves. It was the humans who were sometimes fazed by her.

I was amused when the instructor came up to me at one meeting to say the children were going to do some jumping.

'I don't suppose Pepita can jump, so Max needn't go in this,' she said kindly.

'Pepita *can* jump,' I told her, trying not to smile as I thought of how she could jump out of her paddock whenever she felt like a change of scene. Interestingly, although fences of any sort were never a barrier to her, she never went over, or through, a boundary fence, even though she moved with us to several different properties during her life. I often wondered how she knew.

It was at a donkey club trail ride that she showed just how she could jump. Max and I were in the Blackwood Forest. There were about ten donkeys, mostly fairly large Australian donkeys ridden by adults. I had taken my pony mare, Peppi, and another woman had also brought a pony.

We were unloading and saddling up when I heard a man asking, 'Where is the mule?' I looked round to see who was speaking and why. I hoped he wasn't raising an objection.

Max had no such qualms and called to him. 'Here; she is here.'

A man came forward smiling, his eyes

on Pepita. 'I heard a mule was coming so I've come along to see her,' he told us. 'She is smaller than I expected—and prettier.' Max and Pepita both looked pleased at this comment. 'How do you think she will go?'

'She'll be great,' Max told him confidently.

'Have a good day,' he said as we prepared to ride off. 'I'll come back at the end of the day and see how she's managed.'

The first obstacle we came across on our day's ride was a fairly wide but shallow creek of wonderfully clear water. There was a row of quite large stones across the most shallow point. Stepping-stones designed for human feet. This was the first time I saw Pepita blend her horse and donkey nature into, I suppose, mule, to deal with the situation. Donkeys do not like water, and most of them took a good deal of persuasion to cross, searching for the dry footing of the larger stones to avoid getting their dainty hooves wet. Horses on the other hand are seldom worried about water, so my little mare and the other pony sloshed happily through. Pepita looked at it, and I thought she was going to act like a donkey and say, *Impossible!* But no, having checked out the situation, she crossed faster than anyone, nimbly placing her feet wherever seemed best, on the stones or in the water. I was impressed.

The next drama, which I thought at one point was going to be a fatality, occurred when the track we were following narrowed, and at the same time became very steep. The land fell away at the side of it, leaving a sheer drop of several metres down to the creek we had crossed earlier. Now it was narrower and deeper and flowing faster. We all agreed to negotiate the path on foot and lead our mounts. Except Max, who scornfully said he wasn't getting off, as Pepita could manage this easily. This was correct, and she disappeared from sight up the track. I followed the donkeys leading Peppi. Worried that her friend had gone on ahead and was out of sight, the old mare didn't pay proper attention to where her feet were going. One hoof slipped on the loose stones of the narrow track, this was followed by the whole pony. She was now lying on her side, with me hanging desperately onto the bridle and urging her to calm down. She had gone into complete emotional meltdown and was in serious danger of rolling down the steep embankment to the rocky creek bed several feet below if she didn't stop threshing about in panic mode.

'Max!' I yelled desperately, some instinct telling me that only Pepita could save the day, and Peppi. 'Bring Pepita back!'

To my enormous relief, within seconds they reappeared above us. Max stared in horror at the sight of Peppi, who had totally lost her cool, she was balanced on her side on the path which was little more than a narrow ledge, the only thing keeping her there was the bridle. I hung desperately onto the reins but if it broke or slipped off her head there was nothing I or anyone else could do to save her. My calling for Pepita was a totally instinctive call for help. I just hoped that the sight of her friend might calm the emotional and frightened pony sufficiently to help herself. I don't think I really expected Pepita to actually do anything.

With Max still aloft, she moved to the extreme edge of the track, peered down, sized up the situation and did the only possible thing: talked Peppi out of her predicament. When I say *talked* I mean exactly that. Not her raucous bray but a steady monologue of soft knuckerings which I was sure translated into something like, *Now calm down—you are not going to fall; think about where to put your feet and get up. Then all you have to do is scramble up this bit of a bank to me and you will be quite safe.*

The astonishing thing was that is exactly what Peppi did. She stopped her useless and dangerous threshing about, scrambled to her feet and negotiated the path 'til she was standing safely by Pepita. It was the most amazing example of understanding and loving communication between two animals I had ever seen. My legs were so shaky I felt unable to get on Peppi immediately, but Pepita and Max were heading off up the hillside, and I was as anxious as my overly emotional mount not to let them get out of sight.

It was one of the toughest rides I had ever been on. The hills were many and steep, and all the donkey riders had to get off at one point or another simply because the donkeys, being canny creatures, flatly refused to carry their riders up the steepest parts of the track. The other pony rider and I got off and led our mounts down. They carried us up well enough but felt as if they were going to fall on their noses on the steepest downward bits. I didn't want Peppi to repeat her earlier performance with me aloft! Max stayed on Pepita, both up hill and down.

After a lunch break (we had carried packs of sandwiches with us), we continued on the circular ride back to base, when we came across another obstacle. A large tree blocked our way. An insurmountable barrier I thought, and so apparently did everyone else, for we all dismounted to lead our animals into the rather dense scrub round it.

'I'm not getting off,' Max announced. 'Pepita can jump that.'

I gazed in horror at my small son, and as I did so, Pepita seemed to shrink and the barrier get bigger. 'Don't be silly, it's much too big,' I squeaked, adding in what I hoped was a convincing manner, 'We are all getting off and leading them round it through the bush.'

'Huh!' It was a scornful sound followed by a confident, 'Pepita can do it.' And before I could say any more, he said to Pepita, 'Can't you? Come on; show them!'

It was a heart-stopping moment. I stood rooted to the spot and watched as she cleared the fallen tree with, it seemed, barely a centimetre to spare, and landed safely on the other side. Her triumphant young rider beamed. 'Told you she could do it.' No one else was game to follow his example.

When we arrived back at base our mule admirer, true to his word, was there to greet us. Max enjoyed giving him a blow-by-blow account of the day and Pepita's handling of the obstacles, finishing with a proud, 'I never had to get off once!'

My eyes had been opened to the caring character of this wonderful little mule, and through her I got a glimpse of the love and friendship so many animals had for each other, and felt the first stirrings of unease about the manner in which we, in our all powerful role, ignored these and casually broke relationships with our arrogant human assumption that as mere animals they were not capable of such feelings.

Chapter Seven

After her successful day with the Donkey Club in the Blackwood Forest, Max asked if he could take Pepita to Pony Club. 'She can do anything a pony can do,' he assured me.

I couldn't deny that, after all, Pepita had risen to the challenges presented by the donkey club better than the ponies. So off she went to Pony Club, and proved Max right. Anything a horse could do, she could do better. We discovered that she loved the social life these outings presented, and if for any reason she wasn't included, she would run up and down the fence making the welkin (whatever that is) ring with her cries of, 'Hey what about me?'

We were at Pony Club one afternoon; I was chatting to a group of parents on one side of the ground and Max and Pepita were working in their class on the other. It was a fairly large ground and a fairly large Pony Club. Suddenly everything stopped and the only sound to be heard was Pepita's voice. I knew no other creature with a voice like that, or as loud. There was no mistaking it or looking the other way and pretending it was nothing to do with me. Rooted to the spot, I stared across the ground in horror; she was coming towards me as fast as possible, scattering children, ponies and parents in all directions. Max was still aloft but I could see it was Pepita, not him, in control. They came to an abrupt halt at my side, effectively scattering the group of people I was talking to.

'Whatever . . .' I began, but breathlessly explaining.

'It's her tail . . .' he gasped. 'She swished it and it got caught in the crupper buckle. Can you unhook it? I tried, but she wouldn't let me. She insisted on coming to you. '

Before he had finished explaining the problem I saw it myself; it was only the work of a second to put the matter right. Had she allowed him, Max could have done it himself, without even getting off.

'Thanks! I couldn't stop her coming—but she didn't run into anyone. She didn't do anything wrong. I'll go back into class now.'

Pepita gave my arm a nudge with her muzzle before she turned round and trotted demurely, and silently, back across the ground to her class.

I watched her go, slightly bemused; I found I was rubbing my arm where she had nudged me. I knew that this was her way of thanking me and reassuring me that all was well.

Disrupted classes were going again, and on the other side of the ground I could see Pepita working out calmly. I found it hard to believe that such a short time ago she had caused mayhem in this peaceful and orderly scene. I turned back to the group of people I had been talking to before we were interrupted and saw the pony club boss walking towards me

Oh dear! I thought, remembering that she had only been admitted to Pony Club on condition she didn't upset the horses. *This is it—she is going to ask me to take my unruly mule*

away. I looked around for an escape route, but there was none. I had no alternative but to stay put. Then, as she reached me, I realised she was beaming at me. She did not look annoyed at all.

'That was amazing!' she exclaimed, smiling broadly.

'Just what I was thinking,' one of the parents agreed.

I looked round at them; they were all smiling.

I was still wondering what was so amazing and how to respond when another parent chipped in. 'The confidence she has in you—like a kid knowing Mum could fix it.'

'Yes,' I murmured, somewhat confused. Here I was expecting brickbats, and yet it seemed I was getting bouquets. Then what they were saying sunk in and I felt a warm glow, and I too smiled broadly. They were right, it *was* amazing. I had finally won her trust, and in return I knew I could trust her too.

Chapter Eight

The word mule drew me like a magnet whenever I saw it in one of the equestrian magazines. Two articles appeared about this time, one in *The Australian Hoofs & Horns* about teams of mules who performed annually at one of the big Agricultural Shows in South Africa. I have forgotten what exactly they did, but I have remembered something the writer said: *'Mules are the only animal other than chimpanzees who really understand applause and are not frightened by it. On the contrary, the louder the applause the better they perform.'* This was interesting; I knew horses were afraid of applause. As a teenager I had been in an event at a horse show and at the end all the competitors were lined up in front of the grandstand and given a round of applause. Without exception all our horses, most of them seasoned performers, backed away from the clapping.

The other was in an American magazine devoted to donkeys and mules, and gave instructions for teaching them to put their front feet up on a pedestal.

What it didn't say was that *Safety First* was the motto of these intelligent long-ears. I got a large log and up-ended it as a pedestal. Pepita inspected it carefully, nudging it with her muzzle. It had a slight wobble and she instantly backed away, looking at me with rolling eyes. We levelled off the base and I tried again. This time she cautiously put one hoof on it when requested. It was slightly damp and her hoof slipped. Again her reproachful expression made it clear she didn't consider it safe. So we tacked a piece of old carpet on the top.

She tested it carefully, and then up she went. She was rather proud of this achievement, or perhaps she liked the enhanced view, and it was soon easier to get her up on her pedestal than down. She never failed to check that it did not wobble and her foot did not slip before she mounted it. This impressed me, also her willingness to learn this with the proviso it must be safe.

I also read in an American magazine that one of the things that made mule performance classes in American shows so popular was the unpredictability of mules. A popular class was high jumping. In this, the mule was not ridden but jumped from a stand still and went on with the jump increasing in height, and entrants being eliminated when they failed, until there was only one left in.

It was not unusual for the mule who had been the star all day to stand there and look at its handler with an expression on its face that said all too clearly *'I have no idea what you want me to do!'* I thought this very amusing, until Pepita pulled the same trick on me.

The local paper had recently reviewed my book, *Donkeys, Ponies & Mules—Their Care and Training,* and a reporter was sent out to get a story on the donkeys and how we used them. He was also instructed to get a photo of Pepita on her pedestal.

It was a hot humid day in mid-summer, the sort when tempers can run short, so I was ready for the reporter when he arrived. The donkeys were in the stable yard, and Pepita and her pedestal in the round yard. This was a special training yard with high wooden walls and a sand base, which kept the pedestal stable. The reporter arrived on time and said he would take the photo of Pepita first as he had been told to be sure he got it. I don't think he should have said this within range of her long ears, and I jokingly mentioned this when she put on her silly ass expression when I asked her to step up. I received a withering look from the young man, conveying all too clearly that Pepita wasn't the only stupid one here. I repeated my request, and again, and again, with ever increasing firmness and urgency. Pepita continued to look blank.

'Look,' I pleaded desperately after fifteen minutes that seemed like forty, 'can't you use the photo of her that is in the book?'

'No!' he snapped. 'I have been told I must get a photo of her actually doing it.' I got the impression that this was to prove that she really did this and we had not hoisted her up there to photograph her for the book. Pepita gave me a vigorous nudge; I turned to look at her and could have sworn there was a twinkle in her eye. Whatever—I knew the nudge meant she was enjoying the situation.

'Come and photograph the donkeys,' I urged, acting on a sudden inspiration. He started to repeat his spiel that he had to get this photo of her. 'I can't go back without it,' he told me, his voice shaking with despair. I hustled him out,

'Just do the donkeys—first,' I suggested, my voice scarcely above a whisper when I hoped we were out of Pepita's orbit. He looked at me suspiciously, convinced now that I was, to put it delicately, quite mad.

He photographed the donkeys, all were pleasantly co-operative, and all the time Pepita brayed from the round yard. He managed to ask me in the lulls while she drew breath for the next assault on our ears, if it was *that mule* making the noise and if so why.'

'She is mad because you are giving attention to the donkeys,' I told him. 'She will probably be okay when we go back in and you'll get your photo.'

'I hope so,' he said fervently, obviously thinking this assignment was proving more dangerous than expected.

I was right. When I opened the door of the round yard the word 'Up!' was barely out of my mouth and Pepita was standing there with her front feet in place—on the pedestal.

Chapter Nine

Pepita's confidence that I would make things right when her tail got caught up in the crupper was not an isolated instance. I was to discover, in her view, that we were there for each other. I had recently purchased a new donkey jack, and he was in the paddock with Pepita when for some unexplained reason, maybe he was just feeling grumpy, he walked up to her as she grazed and bit her at the top of her hind leg. I saw it happen and knew she had done nothing to provoke him. She turned and saw me at the fence and called me, standing on three legs very piteously. Worried that she might have been seriously hurt I scrambled through the fence and hurried over to her. She held out the bitten leg to me.

I rubbed the spot where he had bitten her; the skin was not broken so I said, 'There, there,' in soothing tones as I rubbed. 'Better now,' I assured her in the sort of syrupy voice one would use to a child who has just had a painful but not serious injury kissed better. Down went the leg and she took an experimental step forward. Yes—it was better! She gave me one of her special nudges and walked forward a few steps to make sure.

Two years into the happy partnership between Max and Pepita, their relationship broke up. Looking back I can see it was time. Nothing lasts forever, Max was growing tall and Pepita was only twelve hands. In their two years together each had learned a lot; it was hard to say whether Max had learned more from Pepita or she from him. The surprising thing was that it was Pepita who ended the partnership.

They had gone off happily for a ride, just the two of them. I was surprised to see them turning in at the gate only fifteen minutes later.

'You are back very quickly,' I commented. 'What happened?' There was something about the way they both looked that told me that something had.

'We quarrelled,' he told me.

'Quarrelled?' I tried to hide my amusement at his choice of word. 'What happened?'

'When we got to the fork in the road she wanted to go one way and I wanted to go the other.'

'So . . .?' I probed. I knew that Pepita often expressed her preference for a particular route, but it was just that, she let you know she would prefer to go somewhere else but never insisted.

'I hit her,' he admitted, and I noticed he was carrying a riding stick.

'And what did she do then?' I asked. Obviously it was nothing too serious for he was still in the saddle in one piece. But I knew

43

Pepita had what amounted to a phobia about sticks, and wondered why he had taken it, as he was also aware of this.

'She brought me home. I couldn't make her go in any direction but home.'

And that was it. She would never do anything for him again. So I gave up Peppi the grey mare I always rode myself and who was a good hand taller than Pepita.

'I suppose,' I said doubtfully, looking at the little mule in front of me who I hadn't been on since that disastrous first ride, 'I could ride Pepita.'

By the greatest of good fortune for both of us I read a story in an American magazine about a man, a normal sized man, who was riding a mule at show-jumping events round America and frequently winning. Nothing so surprising about that but his mule was only twelve hands—exactly the same size as Pepita. If he could do that, there was nothing to stop me, a normal size woman, riding Pepita. So I did, and our relationship grew and deepened. I had been brought up with horses and had a donkey stud for many years, but Pepita was teaching me all the time, and as she did so our relationship was deepening and growing. Her personality was so big it overshadowed her small stature, and in all the years I rode her and all the things we did together, I never felt I was riding a small animal.

I began to feel that *someone out there* was

putting just the right reading matter in front of me when I needed it. This was not the first time and it would not be the last. I dipped my lid mentally in thanks to whoever it was.

Remembering her reaction, I never carried a stick when I rode her. When I bought her I was told she was completely untrained, but in a later conversation her breeder said that she had a man in to train her young ponies and that she had hoped to get Pepita trained to harness but it was hopeless.

We also had an idea that she would be good pulling a cart. We had trained several of our donkeys and found them very good. In fact we used one, Sally, regularly to feed out hay to the cattle, and found it more efficient than a tractor. She walked out up the paddocks *going* and *whoaing* on a verbal command, and came back at a smart pace with the cart empty, except for the driver. All Sally's gear would have fitted Pepita, so we thought she could take over when Sally was on maternity leave. But all our attempts to get her even close to the cart failed. She went into total meltdown. I tried placing a bowl of food in the cart but she would not touch it. The Donkey Club had several driving members and we often had rides when two or three people drove harness donkeys. Pepita freaked out completely if one came near her. We gave up the idea of training her and concentrated on getting her to accept carts pulled by other animals. Every weekend my daughter drove her sensible little donkey and I rode Pepita. It was many weeks before I could ride close enough to the cart to be able to have a conversation.

I was sure that while it was true that she was completely untrained when I bought her, it was not the whole truth. Someone had tried, resulting in a very bad experience for her involving a cart. Maybe her stick phobia was connected. Her owner must have known about this and that was why she was offered to me. There was no doubt she loved her dearly, but her many years of experience would have told her that the future for a mule with a flawed reputation was a dog meat can. She wanted her to have a chance of a better future, and for some reason she believed I could give it to her.

I accepted that if she would go on a ride and not panic if a donkey pulling a cart passed her, I was happy. She was busy enough in her new role as my special mount, and I had Sally if I wanted to drive. As for sticks, I never carried one when I rode her, nor did I ever feel the need for one.

At this time I was taking people on trail rides and also giving riding lessons to complete beginners. Because Pepita was now so good, I thought I could use her to do this. This was when I found out what her breeder had meant when she said she would know if Pepita liked me. She made it very clear that she did not like some people and they simply could not get on her. With those she did like, she behaved angelically. When I watched her would-be riders end up sitting on the ground instead of on her back, I had no idea what she had done because to an onlooker she did not appear to do anything, certainly nothing violent. My mind went back down the years and I remembered the little mule in the Blackpool circus. Whatever she did it was the same; I think it must be a trick of dropping the shoulder and throwing the person off balance at the moment when they take one foot off the ground. But I honestly don't know. The unfortunate person would inevitably end up sitting on the ground while Pepita stood back from them and rolled her eyes in a way I was learning meant she did not like something about a situation. In this case it was usually the would-be rider.

There was nothing for it but to suggest they tried another mount when this happened. I was only thankful that she did nothing in the least violent, and after a few demonstrations of this skill, which I found embarrassing, I gave up using her to teach beginners and always rode her myself when we left the home paddocks for a trail ride. She was far the best mount I had for this. Sally, my biggest donkey, who at nearly thirteen hands was taller than Pepita, was excellent, but did not want to take the lead. Without someone in front of her she was apt to hang back and say to the one

47

behind her *'After you, dear.'* Two of our older ponies, Peppi and Molly, on the other hand were a nightmare if on the same ride together with inexperienced riders. Both coveted the lead position, and it soon degenerated into a race if they felt they, and not their rider, was in charge. Pepita was happy to take any position in the ride. This meant I could lead it, bring up the rear or ride anywhere among the other riders. It is important that the people in charge should be able to do this without doing constant battle with their own mounts.

This small business taught me a lot about horses. It wasn't enough to have X number of horses for the same number of riders. It was vitally important to match personalities. When a person told me she was the most experienced rider of the group and began counting the times she had ridden on her fingers, I knew Molly was not the horse for her. This wonderful old mare simply took charge of people with an exaggerated idea of their own horsemanship skills and decided to cut them down to size. Fairy on the other hand was so kind and considerate to beginners that simply by watching her I could tell exactly how much experience a rider had. She refused to move from a walk to a trot unless she felt her rider was secure, or from a trot to a canter. Yet, this same horse could give a good rider a superb day out and was a wonderful jumper.

There is an old saying that *Those who*

need to learn teach. Certainly when I set out to teach the rudiments of horsemanship to total beginners I learned more true horse knowledge than I had amassed to date, and much credit for this must go to Pepita who was such an undemanding partner I was free to observe and learn.

Chapter Ten

Pepita's skills as an escape artist would rival the legendary Houdini. She could jump over most fences, but she often chose to go through them instead. I don't mean she crashed through leaving a broken fence behind; no, she wriggled and crawled through amazingly quickly, leaving no damage.

This applied to electric fences as well. On one occasion I was standing with a visitor when Pepita decided to exit the small holding paddock through the electric fence. She seemed to sort of fold herself up, and seconds later was on the other side.

'Your electric fence isn't working,' my visitor told me.

'I'm pretty sure it is.'

'It can't be. That mule just got through it.'

He was so convinced that I was wrong and he was right that he put his hand on it. Not for long though. With an almighty yell and some choice oaths he jumped back.

'I told you it was working,' I said and could not refrain from grinning broadly. I was sure Pepita on the other side of the fence was joining in the joke as well.

'How the devil did she do that?' he wondered aloud. 'Those fences pack a punch,' he added ruefully, rubbing his hand. 'I suppose being a mule she has a tough, insensitive skin,' he decided.

I let him think that to salve his ego, but I knew that her skin was so sensitive that I had to get special mohair string girths for her as anything else chafed her badly. I also knew she had incredible hearing—those long ears were not just ornaments—and probably picked her moment to go through between pulses.

The surprising thing was that though she could move about the property at will, she never went through a boundary fence. We moved four times and not once did she ever leave home. I wonder how she knew the borders. If you or I were in the same position and did not see a map of the property, and couldn't read anyway, and never saw the place 'til we were transported there, I doubt if we could equal her skill. There must have been something about these fences that distinguished them from the interior ones, but I have no idea what it was.

For a time we were breeding Pinto Ponies and had a very handsome bay and white skewbald stallion. Pepita liked him very much, and when she was in season would often put herself in his paddock. But Sunny liked to keep his mares in a group, which presented a problem for her, as once in with him he didn't like her to leave. Any mare wandering from the group was firmly rounded up. She would watch for me going down the drive and make a dash for the gate. I had to be quick opening it and shutting it again, for Sunny would gallop up at full speed if he saw she was making her escape. I co-operated with her and often called her name to let her know I was on my way down the drive to give her a chance of a head start on him. We had some exciting moments as I unlatched the gate and she dashed through, and I only just got it shut before he thundered up. But we managed it; Pepita usually got through, and I never let Sunny out.

Mules are a hybrid that theoretically should not exist, as horses and donkeys have a different number of chromosomes and mules are always sterile. Not all mare, or molly, mules come in to season, but Pepita did. Male or jack mules have a reputation for being very randy, but like the females they too are sterile. Big horse breeding concerns sometimes ran an entire jack mule with their mares as he would tell them when a mare was in season but could not get her in foal. It has been said that an uncastrated male mule is one of the most dangerous and useless animals alive due to his

51

strong sex drive coupled with his infertility. It is probably because maternal instinct, a facet of the sex drive, is often strong in mare mules that many people prefer them. Certainly as the bond between us increased, Pepita's care for me was often quite motherly.

Mules also have the reputation, like elephants, for never forgetting. It was this quality no doubt that explained her attitude to sticks and carts. She probably felt when Max carried a stick and actually used it, that it was a betrayal of their mutual trust. Whatever it was she never forgave him.

I was helping my husband and another man move a mob of sheep one day. Because there were a lot of well grown lambs in the flock they were not as tractable as a batch of old ewes. Pepita was excellent working sheep and it was normally a pleasant and not at all taxing job for me, as she would work them almost like a dog and could walk at sheep's trotting pace. The two men had sticks, which I told them were quite unnecessary with Pepita on the job, and pointed out that she did not like them.

My husband who had seen Pepita at work with sheep before, somewhat reluctantly discarded his. The other man, who was convinced a good stick was essential to move a mob of sheep, did not. Pepita and I eyed him warily, and I could tell her attention was as much on him as on the job at hand. The only ones winning were the sheep. They probably noted this too and made a dash for freedom. My husband picked up his discarded stick and both men leaped wildly in front of the sheep, sticks and arms brandishing in the time-honoured way of men trying to control sheep without the help of a good dog, or in this instance, mule. Pepita threw up her head, eyes rolling, and instead of being a help, backed away. I attempted to save face by looking as if this was my idea, but my fury was genuine.

'I told you not to wave sticks about!' I yelled 'Well you can manage on your own, because Pepita won't do it, and I certainly can't make her while you are waving those bloody great sticks in her face!'

The men looked somewhat startled at my outburst, but good sense prevailed. They both knew it was going to take them a great deal longer to get the sheep where they were supposed to be without Pepita's (and my) help. The sticks were put aside, the yelling and the waving arms reduced and the sheep successfully corralled.

I did work cattle with her but she was not so good with them. After all, some of them were bigger than her, and a recalcitrant steer can be intimidating. On these occasions we both decided discretion was the better part of valour and I sought Molly's help instead.

This old skewbald mare had only one eye (we always said she saw more with that than other horses with two). I had bought her for my eldest son when he was nine years old, from a dealer who had bought her from the killers—the dog meat people. This dealer bought at horse sales, not when they were in the ring but after they had been knocked down for this fate. She had an uncanny eye for a horse, and when she saw one that she felt deserved a better future, would offer the dog meat people a quick profit and buy them to resell. Molly was one of these, and she proved one of the best investments in horseflesh I ever made. She had so much experience behind her and knew so much that she was greatly responsible for making my son the horseman he is today. He did Pony Club with her where she proved she had obviously done it all before, and when it came to stock work she was unbeatable, never fazed by any steer, however awkward. She lived with us for many years until she dropped dead in her home paddock.

I remember her with affection and admiration and sadness at the thought that so many like her, with so much experience and wisdom, are thrown out like so much garbage when they should have years of useful life ahead of them. The saying *Young children need old horses* is very true.

Chapter Eleven

'You have what?' I asked my caller, somewhat ungraciously and ungrammatically.

'I have an animal casting agency and I have been asked to find a mule for a film,' the pleasant voice on the other end of the line repeated. 'I understand you have one?'

'Yes—I have,' I replied cautiously, wondering if this were some sort of hoax.

'Crawford Productions are making a full length film about the *Sullivans,* it's set in Yugoslavia . . .' At this point I was convinced someone was playing a joke. I couldn't take Pepita to Yugoslavia. 'That is the *story* is set there but they are filming it on Mount Macedon.'

'Oh.' I was getting more confused by the minute.

'The terrain is right you see. It's about freedom fighters or something camping in the forest on the mountain.'

'What do they need a mule for?' It sounded as if she didn't know a great deal more about it than I did. 'What will she be expected to do?'

'Oh she won't have to actually do anything, just be part of the background, make it look authentic,' she explained, adding hastily, 'You will be paid of course.'

So Pepita launched into the film business.

She was required to do two days, and it was true, she didn't actually have to do anything. Being tethered and eating, two activities she excelled at, could hardly be called performing.

My elder son, who was then a well built and physically strong fifteen year old, came with me, which was fortunate, or Pepita's brief film career would have ended before it began.

The station wagon chugged up the steep mountain track, and I prayed that the weight of the horse float behind it with its precious passenger would not start rolling backwards, and we duly arrived at the film site at the time instructed.

I parked the horse float and led Pepita down the ramp. She was only wearing a simple nylon headstall, which was ideal for travelling and also to tether her. I had parked in such a way that as she stepped out of the float down the ramp she was looking straight ahead to the panoramic view. I tried to turn her at the bottom of the ramp to hitch her securely to the outside of the float. No way—her eyes took on a faraway look as she gazed somewhere into the distance, and she just kept walking. When it came to physical strength it was no contest between us. I was being dragged, my feet sliding on the loose stones of the path, painfully aware of the inadequate control the head collar gave me and conscious that far from slowing down, we were actually speeding up.

Just as I was sure I would have to let go, and wondering where Pepita intended to end up, my son heard my anguished cry for help and came to the rescue. He grabbed her head collar on the other side with both hands and as each of us hung on desperately and implored her to '*WHOA!*' she stopped walking and came to a halt. She also seemed to come out of her trance-like state and return to an awareness of her surroundings. I was relieved to get one of her reassuring nudges.

My son pointed out that had she continued her determined march down the hill she would have been very close to her birthplace. The property where she was born was very near the foot of Mount Macedon. It seemed a fanciful theory, yet the more I thought about it the more I thought it was correct. But how did she know? That was a question I asked many times over the years when she seemed to display a knowledge that, theoretically, was hidden from her.

There was a bit more excitement before the day's filming started. Six sheep were also required, all they had to do was be penned in a temporary corral. One escaped en route from the trailer they arrived in to the makeshift pen, and it disappeared immediately among the trees. Everyone watched in horror, convinced only five would go home when the owner came to collect them. One of the cameramen abandoned his gear and vanished in hot pursuit. We wondered if we would ever see him again, but in a very short time he reappeared, the sheep (a full grown one, not a lamb) slung across his shoulders, its forelegs firmly held by one hand and its hind legs by the other. We all gaped, lost in admiration, and I wondered how he had got it up there by himself.

The cameraman, a young Maori, fit and of splendid physique, brushed our admiration aside modestly, saying it was nothing. He had been brought up on a sheep station in the South Island and had been handling sheep since he could walk. The woman from the casting agency in charge of the animals was weeping tears of relief and gratitude. Most of us had heard the owner lecturing her on their value and instructing her not to let them escape before he left them with her.

The hero of this drama looked embarrassed and repeated, 'It was nothing—I've been handling sheep all my life,' before taking up his camera. With the sheep safely penned and Pepita on her tether, filming began.

It was bitterly cold up there on the mountain. Those not actively involved huddled gratefully round a large bonfire. The cast were all wearing flannelette pyjamas beneath their costumes and had thick coats to huddle into between scenes.

There was a large mobile kitchen which served morning coffee and afternoon tea, and in between, a sumptuous hot lunch. Pepita behaved perfectly after her early lapse. Being tethered and enjoying the 'Yugoslavian' smorgasbord was not taxing. She earned fifty dollars a day for that, as well as an excellent lunch for us. This was over thirty years ago and seemed like money for jam. I had fantasies of a film career for her while we lived off her earnings. Alas it was not to be.

She did have other chances to perform however. At that time I had a saddle shop specializing in the best gear for donkeys, mules and small ponies, and I was asked to give a talk to the Donkey Club. As it was an outdoor event I took Pepita along as my model. She did the job perfectly with obvious enjoyment, standing by me without being tied up while I talked and patiently having the different saddles fitted on her and taken off again. When I concluded, my audience broke into spontaneous applause, more for her than me. By this time I had taught her, among other things to bow, so I suggested to her that she should show her appreciation of the audience by bowing. This she did, and the audience, delighted, clapped even harder.

Pepita bowed again, deeper and deeper— the clapping increased—she bowed again. So it went on. Pepita was totally carried away and quite deaf to my entreaties to her to stop bowing. Eventually I had to beg the audience to stop applauding her, and she finally stopped.

I reflected that what I had read about mules understanding applause appeared to have some truth in it—for Pepita at least.

Chapter Twelve

One of the things Pepita taught me was the value and power of a loving friendship. Not just in the gift of her friendship to me but with her equine friends. One of these was with Feather/Fleur. Her, or rather their story was one very suggestive of reincarnation. We had bought a lovely little black and white pinto mare with a pretty filly foal at foot, and in foal again to a pinto stallion. It was not a sensible buy; I bought with my heart not my head. They had no papers, there was no record of the father of her foal, or of the stallion the mare was in foal to. The only information we had was standing before us in the shape of Maggie and her foal, who we called Feather. The little mare didn't actually have a name, even though she was middle-aged, when we bought her from a dealer. But it turned out to be a very good purchase. Maggie, short for Magpie, as we called her, was a remarkable personality as well as being very well educated.

Feather was not only extremely pretty she was very unusual. Buckskin and white, with a black tail that looked as if it had been given to her at the last moment, grabbed at random from the cupboard where tails were kept when new foals were kitted out. I had never seen a pony this colour before.

Magpie and her daughter proved to be delightful to know. They both had excellent temperaments and when the mother had a break from maternal duties we also found she had been very well trained at some point in her life. Feather grew from a pretty foal to a beautiful pony with a lovely temperament like her mother, and in due course we trained her for the children to ride.

Pepita loved Feather but we didn't realise how much until tragedy struck. Feather met with a mysterious accident, a blow to the head, that left her staggering and reeling into things. We put her in a stable and called the vet. He could do little other than advise us to keep her in the stable with plenty of straw to protect her as she seemed to have lost all her natural balance. As we stood looking over the half door of her stable, heartbroken to see our lovely and much loved pony in this state, and getting worse as we watched, Pepita joined us in our vigil. Somehow she knew that her friend was in trouble and found her way from whichever paddock she had been in to the stable yard. She was still there early next morning, just outside the half door. Feather had lost consciousness and died a short while later. We were all, including Pepita, heartbroken. She, like us, had loved Feather and had been her close friend for most of her life.

What followed then was very strange. We had a lovely grey mare, Fairy, who had three foals by different coloured stallions. All had been grey, so we presumed that she was what is known as *pure for grey*. Such mares have two grey parents and whatever colour the stallion will always have grey foals.

Shortly after Feather's tragic death we put Fairy in the paddock with our bay and white pony stallion, but we didn't think she conceived. For most of the following year we still thought that. In fact it was on the principle of better safe than sorry rather than a conviction that she was actually in foal that made us put her in the security and privacy of the foaling paddock, a small paddock with no obvious hazards, very close to the house.

It was slightly more than a year after Feather's death. I was getting breakfast and my husband was outside doing early morning chores. When he came in I thought he had completed them very quickly.

'Fairy has foaled,' he told me. There was something about his voice that made me look at him anxiously.

'Is she—are they—all right?' I asked.

'They are both fine,' he assured me, 'but you must come out—now—and look at the foal.'

There was something in his voice that still had me worried in spite of his words so I downed tools and followed him.

My husband broke the silence as we leaned on the fence staring at the new arrival.

'It's Feather—back again.' He spoke in low, awed tones as if he was in church. All I could do was stare at the pretty foal staggering towards us on legs she wasn't quite sure how to work yet.

When I found my voice, all I could say was, 'She knows us.' For her behaviour was most unusual in a newborn foal. Fairy found it so too, and kept calling to her in low urgent tones and trying to nudge her back against her flank where such a new baby should be. This lovely foal born a year after Feather's death was a complete replica of her. The same buckskin and white colouring, even the same black tail. We called her Fleur. She kept up this unusual behaviour of wanting to socialise with us for several days and never showed any of the normal wariness of humans that is normal in newborn foals. Fairy, although she was a very friendly pony, obviously felt this behaviour not only odd but possibly dangerous, and called her back and walked over to her trying to nudge her away from us.

'Do you think—could she possibly be . . .?' we asked one another. Pepita had no doubts; she loved her and was her friend and protector always, just as she had been to Feather. It was as if she picked up their relationship where it had been abruptly broken.

When I look through old photos I find it hard to tell which is Feather and which Fleur and have to look for other clues. It was almost as if one were a negative photographic image, the buckskin colouring on their heads was on the left side of the face on one and the right on the other. But this was no help in working out whose photo it was unless you could remember which one it was. So I went by another clue, the size of the children in the photo. My younger son had ridden Feather, but by the time Fleur was old enough to ride he had grown far too tall for a pony her size and my daughter rode her.

The four of us, Ruth and Fleur, Pepita and I, rode many happy miles together in the bush. Pepita was always somewhat edgy alone in the bush, probably because of those four early years when she saw so little of the world. Fleur on the other hand had no such worries and would stride out boldly, giving Pepita confidence.

Sadly, Fleur did not live to make old bones. If the two lives of these lovely and much loved ponies were put together they added up to one average lifespan for a horse.

The first time the vet visited our property after Fleur's surprise arrival, he stood for a long time silently staring at her.

'Extraordinary,' he said as if he couldn't quite believe the evidence of his own eyes. 'In all my years in practice I had never seen a horse that colour until I saw Feather, and now I've seen two.' He paused before adding, almost inaudibly, 'Or have I?'

Chapter Thirteen

Why are we always so amazed when we find animals behaving with what we like to think of as human qualities? Could it be because if we admit to them feeling and expressing love, devotion, grief, the whole gamut of what we like to think of as human emotions, it makes our treatment of them even more reprehensible than it already is? The exception to this is probably the dog; we have come to expect dog-like devotion from the dog as our right as the god-like master being. When we come across similar emotion in other creatures we say they are dog-like.

I will not insult Pepita by saying she was dog-like. She was at all times uniquely herself. It was being an observer of her close friendship with Feather/Fleur that I became aware that my own relationship with her was in some ways quite special. I knew I loved her, and I thought, and hoped, that she liked me, but when I discovered she could pick up messages from me even if we were not physically close, I began to watch myself and her more keenly.

The first time this happened I was riding with my daughter along one of the tracks in the bush that surrounded our property.

'We will turn back at the next bend,' I said. I had a clear picture of the corner, a sharp one, a bit further on in the track. When we reached it Pepita swung round without waiting for instructions. I was pretty sure I had not given her any, but I knew there was always the chance I had inadvertently done so. A slight shift in the saddle maybe, or she could have understood what I said.

But there was no possibility of this when my younger son interrupted my baking one day to ask if I would ride with him.

'Just wait 'til I get these cookies out of the oven, then I will,' I told him, never loathe to exchange an apron for a saddle, adding, 'If you can go and find Pepita and get her into the stable for me, that would be a great help.' As always, I had no idea where on the property she was, or in which paddock.

In a very short time he was back, but my cookies were still in the oven. 'That was quick; she must have been in a paddock close by.'

He grinned. 'Better than that, when I went out I met her at the top of the drive, just turning into the stable yard,' he told me. 'If you are not quite ready I'll saddle her for you.' He turned back at the door and added, 'I think

66

she must have picked up that you wanted her and was coming in.'

I thought so too as I got my baking out of the oven and pulled on my riding boots. When I got outside she was saddled and waiting and greeted me with a soft knucker, so different to her raucous bray, and of course one of her nudges, when I walked up to her.

I realised this communication with her was a two-way thing when I asked her how her rug was constantly getting undone. She loved her winter rug and always took good care of it, not casually running it along a barbed wire fence, as some ponies do, apparently enjoying the noise. I appreciated this; good weatherproof outdoor clothing for horses is expensive. Pepita's lasted many seasons without getting ripped or torn, in spite of scrambling through fences, and she would not dream of going into the dam wearing a rug, as old Molly had done. So I was both surprised and puzzled to find her rug slipping sideways on her because the chest strap was partially or even fully undone. I was pretty sure she could not reach it herself, and even if she could, knew she would not dream of doing anything so foolish.

As I straightened and refastened it for the umpteenth time, I asked her aloud, 'However is this getting undone all the time?' The answer came swiftly. I saw a clear vision in my mind of Fleur picking at the strap with her teeth.

I found it hard to believe that she had actually answered me, but the picture in my head was so clear I decided to act on it. I got a short length of hay band and threaded it through the holes along with the strap and tied it securely in a double knot. I got the usual thank you poke from Pepita before she went to join Fleur in the paddock. I decided to make a point of watching them carefully, and sure enough, it was only the next day when I saw Fleur picking at the strap with her teeth trying to undo it. But my simple solution worked, and so long as I remembered to add a knotted hay-band to the fastening, Pepita's rug stayed in place.

Around the beginning of May was the time the nights began to get cold in our part of the world, and Pepita *told* us she needed her rug. She could get important messages over to my husband as well as myself. I remember my husband joining me for coffee one autumn morning. It was a beautiful sunny day so I had carried it out to the patio.

'Pepita tells me it is time she had her rug on at night,' he told me.

'Yes,' I agreed, 'the nights are getting colder.' I looked at him in surprise. 'What do you mean *she* told you?'

He looked at me over his coffee mug. 'Did I say that?'

I nodded. 'You definitely did. You didn't say *you thought* she should have it on.'

He frowned slightly as he considered this. 'That is what it seemed like; the thought came into my head as if she was saying it, not as if I was consciously thinking about the nights getting colder—I wasn't, I was just appreciating the beautiful day, if I was thinking about the weather at all. But she is right; she probably does get cold at night. Yes—I think she definitely did send me a message and I received it.'

After that, Pepita herself always decided the actual date she started wearing her rug. One or other of us would say, 'Pepita thinks it time to start her rug.' It would be fetched out and dusted down, ready to be put on that night.

Chapter Fourteen

Pepita had a sweet tooth, and not just for biscuits. On one of the properties where she lived with us, there was a wonderful old pear tree in the sheep yard. It seemed an odd place to plant a fruit tree, but there it was, and judging by its size, had been for a good many years. I remember a year when it had an especially good crop, loaded with enormous, very juicy fruit. Pepita was often given one straight from the tree so she was well aware of the source of these delectable delicacies.

We were picking a basketful when someone

held out one to Pepita, who was watching over the fence, expecting her to take a bite from it. Instead, she opened her mouth incredibly wide and the whole pear disappeared. As she closed it, juice streamed from both sides, and her face took on an expression of utter bliss. Having discovered this amazing treat and its source, Pepita took to helping herself whenever she could find a way into the yard. When they grew a bit sparse on the lower branches, she reared up on her hind legs to reach them. There were so many pears we didn't begrudge her enjoying them. There were more than enough for us all to have our share, and we got considerable pleasure just watching her stand up on her hind legs to reach for a ripe pear and seeing her blissful expression when she closed her mouth on it and the juice streamed out.

Unfortunately for Pepita we left this property, but the one we moved to had peach trees, and she was just as partial to a nice juicy peach. We had a total glut of peaches and gave them as treats to ponies and donkeys. It was interesting to see the different way they dealt with the stones. The ponies wuffled them round in their mouths, getting all the fruit off them, and then spat them out. The donkeys, on the other hand, crunched them up. I waited to see what Pepita would do. Unlike the other equines she had no hard and fast rule. Sometimes she spat them out; sometimes she crunched them up.

No doubt she had her reasons but they were not obvious.

I pandered to her sweet tooth, and whenever I had a coffee out, I would slip the lumps of sugar placed in the saucer into my pocket, and bring them home for her. I don't take sugar in coffee or tea, and in those days the sweetener provided in cafés was usually in lump form, not as today, in those little paper cylinders. When I got home I would go out to Pepita's paddock and scratch my thumbnail on the sugar lump in my pocket. She could hear this, those long ears were not just ornaments, and she knew what the sound meant and would come up to the fence. Any other ponies and donkeys in the paddock either did not hear it, or did not associate it with a tasty treat. This meant I was not surrounded by other animals looking for these tasty titbits, and was spared the guilt of only having something for Pepita.

I have always maintained that before attributing extra sensory powers to our animal friends, we need to be sure it is not a case of super sensory. Pepita had amazing hearing. Apart from sweet biscuits, she was also very fond of plain cheese crackers, and could hear my thumbnail against one of these in my pocket from an amazing distance. This meant that whenever I wanted, I could get her without arming myself with a lot of titbits and getting all the occupants of the paddock.

I knew from experience that this could be hazardous. I once had an ice-cream carton of oats kicked out of my hand by a donkey who thought she wasn't getting her fair share. I was lucky it was a donkey. They, and mules, aim when they kick, and can kick the eye out of a needle. Horses tend to lash out wildly. I suffered no ill effects; in fact, I was most astonished to see the oats fly out of my hand.

I am inclined to think that the time she knew a large red gum was about to split in half, was an instance of her remarkable hearing rather than Extra Sensory Perception. We had a Donkey & Mule Club meeting at our property one weekend. A morning ride and an afternoon ride were on the agenda, returning to base, the shady yard of our property, for lunch. I hitched Pepita to the fence under a very large and beautiful red Ggm which gave copious shade, and the rest of the party, human and animal, settled to enjoy lunch in the same area. I noticed that she was the only one who seemed unable to relax and enjoy the break.

'What's the matter with Pepita?' asked one of my friends who knew her well enough to know which were her favourite biscuits.

'Nothing, as far as I know. Why?' She had been in excellent form all morning and I had thoroughly enjoyed riding her.

'I brought a whole packet of her favourite biscuits . . .' she held up the opened packet to

72

show me, 'but she won't touch them; she hasn't had one.'

'That is very strange,' I agreed and walked over to Pepita to see if I could see anything obviously amiss.

'You offer her a biscuit, perhaps she will take it from you,' my friend suggested

She took one from the packet and passed it to me. Pepita stepped back until the tie rope was taut, gave a little agitated snort and rolled her eyes, ignoring the biscuit. She remained like this throughout the lunch break, refusing all offers of food and not attempting to graze. I could not understand it. I had often hitched her at this spot before because the big red gum gave so much shade. Other animals hitched up near her were quite relaxed. During the lunch break I walked over to her several times and told her she was being silly in a soothing sort of voice that totally failed to soothe. Quite the reverse in fact; she seemed more agitated when I was with her. It was not until we packed away our lunch things and everyone saddled up again for the afternoon activities that she returned to normal.

The next day Pepita was relaxing in the paddock about a hundred yards away from the place where she had been tied the day before when I came out of the back door of the house. Almost as I did so, there was a creaking, a rending and a crash, and in the still, warm, summer air, the gum tree I had tied her under the day before split in half. The falling part crashed onto the fence in the very spot where she had been. We both watched from opposite sides but about equal distance from it, and simultaneously we turned towards each other. I have never forgotten the look she gave me.

'I told you so!'

The message was as clear as if she had shouted the words in English to me. Astonished, awed, and not a little ashamed of my obtuseness the day before, I walked over to her and solemnly, and very humbly, admitted that it was I, not her, who had been the stupid one. In her bighearted way she accepted my apology with several vigorous nudges.

I have no idea just how she knew the tree would fall as it did, but know she did. At first I attributed it to some extra sensory knowledge, but on reflection, I think it was probably her incredible hearing. She had heard the tree creaking, but that does not make it any less remarkable. Many of us hear and see things, which with the wisdom of hindsight we know we should have taken as a warning. If it was something she heard, she knew what it meant, and the danger.

I remembered an account I had read of a bridge collapsing in a mountain trekking area. A short while before another party of trekkers had taken another route because their hired pack mule had refused to step on it. They obeyed the instructions given in the leaflet provided by the mule owner which said: *Our mules are very well trained, if they refuse to take a path do not try and force them. It means there is danger.* I vowed to take more note of Pepita in future and treat her with more respect.

Chapter Fifteen

I was intrigued when I read about coon hunting on mules in America. It was a fairly long article in an equestrian magazine from the US, which not only described the sport but the type of mules used for this and how they were trained. Coon hunting apparently took place at night with the riders wearing miners' lamps on their helmets. It also took place in farming country with barbed wire fences. All of which sounded like a pretty deadly combination. Riding a mule at night over country crisscrossed with barbed wire hardly sounded like a fun pastime. I read on and all was revealed. The riders dismounted when they came to a wire fence, draped a white cloth over the top strand to make it clearly visible to the mule, crawled through the fence themselves, and then gave the mule the command to jump. Reunited on the same side of the barrier they rode on to the next fence. The mules used were usually fairly small, twelve to thirteen hands, and well trained. I was intrigued by this and decided to add this to Pepita's repertoire.

Of course we have no coons in Australia and no one hunts anything on mules here. No fault of the mules. Any mule person knows that anything a horse can do, a mule can do better. Juanita, the most famous mule in Australia, was refused admittance to the Sydney Hunt Club where she could have been the first foxhunting mule in Australia as well as the first mule to complete the Quilty.

I had no career plans for Pepita when I decided to train her as a coon-hunting mule but I was greatly intrigued and curious to see if she would behave in the same way as the mules I read about.

I already knew of her jumping ability; not only had I witnessed her spectacular leap over the fallen tree on the Donkey Club trail ride but I had also seen her jumping at Pony Club and was well aware of her skill at getting out of paddocks. She had recently jumped a wire fence that went through a small creek and up the bank on the far side.

An almost impassable barrier, but apart from the fact that she was on the wrong side of this, there was the evidence. On one side of the wire fence was a set of small, neat hoof prints and another set on the landing side. It took real judgment and skill to deal with this obstacle. So I had no doubt of her ability to learn this new party trick.

I had no intention of asking her to jump wire; too risky, and she appeared able to do this already. I wanted to see if she behaved during the early stages of training as these mules did. When coon hunting, the mules do not gallop up to the fence and rely on this to give them the necessary compulsion to clear the obstacle, they are taught to jump to a verbal command from a standstill. To achieve the necessary 'spring' they bend the hocks and get so low on their haunches they almost appear to be sitting down.

The training jump is a single, very narrow stick or pole resting on two side supports, but (and here is where mule sense comes in) it must not be placed like a jump used to train show-jumping horses and fall in the direction of the jump, but fall towards the mule so that it does not knock down easily.

This is because the mule (being smart) will usually test it with its chest to see how firm the obstacle really is. From my experience of horses I thought that was a bit far-fetched and put the jump up in the normal way. Pepita pushed her chest on it, and when it fell, stepped daintily over it with an expression that said all too clearly what she thought of *my* intelligence.

I turned the jump round and started over. Once more she tested it with her chest, and when it remained stable, down on her hocks— and over when I gave the command, 'Jump!'

I read that whatever the height of the obstacle, mules never wasted energy, they invariably cleared it with about one centimetre to spare. This was equally true of Pepita, her judgment was amazing, one centimetre clearance whatever its distance from the ground. Once again I remembered the fallen tree; there had been no wasted energy then.

I also found, to my discomfiture, that exactly the same mule humour surfaced. This type of jumping was a popular event at mule shows, I read, and one of the things that made it such a crowd puller was the unpredictability of the mules. The mule that had won yesterday with flair and panache, might, next time in the ring, gaze off into space or turn and look at his handler with an expression that all too clearly said, *I have no idea what you are asking me to do.'*

Pepita was soon very good at this jumping game and we both enjoyed showing off her newly acquired skill, but when she just stood there looking totally blank when I had a reporter there with a camera I could cheerfully have disowned her forever.

How did I actually teach her? Quite easily. I stood by the jump but slightly to the landing side, with a long lead rope attached to her headstall. A slight twitch to the rope, the clear command 'JUMP!' and a lump of sugar on landing, and well within a week she was all set to go coon hunting.

I found it very interesting she should behave in an identical manner to the mules I read about, testing the stability of the jump with her chest and judging the height so accurately. She had quite a repertoire of tricks now; she could shake hands, bow, put her front feet on her pedestal, and jump.

She had a few tricks of her own too. One of them was quite individual. When we had an argument over the direction we should take she would try to kick my heel with her hind hoof, kicking forward in what is known as a cow kick. It gave the very odd impression of a corkscrew under the saddle, which is the only way I can describe it, and was not in any way vicious or designed to hurt. It was simply her way of expressing herself, and was as familiar to me as the nudge on my arm. Having told me she didn't approve of the route we were taking she usually gave in to my wishes. If she felt strongly enough she might do this three or four times before agreeing to do what I wanted.

I found her very receptive to verbal directives and never ever hit her or even carried a stick. In all the many hours I spent on her back I never came off her again after that first disastrous time. This was not a testament to my riding, but more to the good care she took of me. The only time I was perilously near to a fall was because of, not in spite of this.

When she became my regular mount and

no longer went to Pony Club, I experimented with different types of gear for her, as she no longer was expected to wear an English type saddle and a jointed snaffle bit. It was quite difficult getting it right for both of us. A small Western saddle fitted her well but was too small for me. She needed a crupper as she had a fairly low wither, and English saddles are not usually fitted with them, and anyway are not comfortable for working stock. As far as bits and bridles went she never seemed really happy in a jointed snaffle, so after much experimenting I settled on an Australian poley saddle in a youth's size, which fitted her well. It had modest knee rolls so was good when we worked stock and was extremely comfortable. I found that most bridles her size were too tight around her forehead, which was very broad, due no doubt to the amount of brain she had in there, so I had a one-ear bridle made for her. This is just what it sounds like; there is no brow band but it simply slips over one ear. With this I eventually settled on a small Western colt bit. This is a very mild Western bit, and I used a curb strap instead of a chain, which made it even less severe. I always rode her with long reins in the Western style; like a horse trained in this discipline, she would neck rein—that is, turn against the light pressure of the rein against her neck rather than the pull in her mouth. Before I had worked out just what suited us both, I went through a lot of trials. This was easy for me as I had a Saddle Shop at the time, specialising in equipment for donkeys, small ponies and mules.

I was trying out a hackamore on her. This is not actually a bit as there is nothing in the mouth. A strap over the nose, and a chain under the chin are what give control. The strap over the nose is the crucial part as side shanks of metal connect this to the curb chain.

It was a glorious day, the sort that makes one glad to be alive, I was riding Pepita in our largest paddock which sloped slightly down towards the house and buildings, and we were coming down this at a smart canter, only a breath short of a gallop, both enjoying ourselves, when I noticed that the buckle in the strap over the nose had come undone. This meant that I had no effective control over her, as with this undone there would be no pressure on the curb chain. She would not know if I pulled the reins to stop her or even slow her down. With my usual presence of mind I panicked.

'Whoa!' I shouted. And she did, so suddenly that I shot forward on her neck.

The ground looked very close for a moment; she had only to drop her head and I would have pitched forward over it. But she didn't, she kept her neck rigid and I was able to shuffle back into the saddle and continue at a staid walk, slightly shaken but quite unharmed.

I was impressed by her instant response to my verbal request and by her care of me. It would have been so easy for her simply to deposit me on the ground. I trusted her and had confidence that she would care for me in a manner that was almost maternal, as I was to find out.

Chapter Sixteen

Shortly after this I fractured my wrist. It was one of those stupid accidents that should never have happened. I was putting a rug on our pony stallion in the stable yard; my eldest son was holding his head. As I swung the heavy winter rug up onto the pony's back, he stepped sideways towards me. Instinctively, I stepped back, my feet tangled in the rug, and I went down on the concrete surface of the yard among his hooves, with my left arm somehow twisted underneath me.

Sunny was one of those stallions who thought he was superior because he was male. It was not exactly a threatening movement that he made, just one to show me he was the better of us two. He did this sort of thing to my daughter and me, but never to my husband or sons. He actually had a beautiful nature with not a vicious thought in his head; this was proved by the fact that when I ended up in a tangled muddle with the rug and a useless wrist somewhere between his four hooves, he was very careful not to hurt me.

The upshot of this was that I had my arm in plaster for no less than ten weeks, and did not ride Pepita at all in this time, nor did anyone else. With this prolonged rest she might well have been somewhat skittish when I did ride her again. Many horses I knew would have been. With this thought in the back of my head I put off riding her, until, I said, my wrist was stronger. It was a feeble excuse. The truth was that even though I had not been riding at the time and my injury had nothing whatsoever to do with Pepita, I was terrified of getting on her even though I desperately wanted to resume our happy partnership. There's no accounting for the way the mind works at times.

I chose an afternoon when the whole family were out. This with the wisdom of hindsight was incredibly foolish but at the time my main thought was that I didn't want an audience if I chickened out when it came to the point of actually getting into the saddle.

I spent an extra long time grooming her before I put the saddle and bridle on. She must have wondered what the special occasion was, all the time chatting to her and getting encouraging nudges as I did so. Then I led her out of the stable yard and across the drive to the paddock. I stood by her for a moment, gathering my nerve. Afterwards I wondered why I had been so uptight. I should have had more confidence in her if not in myself.

'Pepita,' I finally said, knowing the moment had come; it was now or never. 'I am feeling very fragile indeed. You will have to take good care of me. '

She gave me a nudge so vigorous I found myself staggering, but far from fazing me it encouraged me. I was sure she had understood. I took a deep breath, ignored the odd tremble in my legs, and climbed into the saddle. I sat there for a few moments, while she stood, quite still. This in itself was unusual; normally she stepped forward as soon as she felt me aloft.

Then I spoke to her again; 'Okay,' I told her, 'walk, just walk—slowly.'

She moved forward—slowly and carefully. She had a fairly large vocabulary: walk, trot and canter were all words she knew, as well as steady, which meant drop down a pace from whatever she was doing, and of course, whoa. When I wanted her to go faster I usually said, 'Come on,' accompanied by the clicking sound that is commonly made to make horses go faster.

She took me all round the paddock with the greatest care. There were no arguments about where or how fast we should go, and had she been carrying a box of eggs, none would have sustained even a crack.

When we got back to the gate my legs

had lost their tremor and I was as happily confident as I had ever been, ready to resume our active life together. In fact, my confidence in her was greater than ever before. I felt she had demonstrated to me how much she cared and that she would always, to the best of her ability, look after me.

Back in the stable I unsaddled her and gave her the brushing she always liked when the saddle came off. During the course of this she gave me several kind nudges as if to reassure me of her loving care. I went inside and collected some of the biscuits she loved. Then I turned her out in the paddock and went back in to make myself a cup of coffee and reflect on the enormous strides our relationship had made since my first attempt to ride her.

How glad I was that I had not given up on her. I did not know then that she would soon demonstrate most dramatically just how seriously she felt the need to look after me.

Chapter Seventeen

The ringing of the phone one sunny Sunday morning heralded the introduction of a creature who was literally a *bête noire* in our lives. He brought a whole new dimension to the phrase *the black sheep of the family*.

A friend living in the nearby town had been

given a black lamb, cute, curly and cuddly at the time. Not any more. Brought up on the bottle with no other sheep, he probably thought he was a person, and a very spoiled one at that. He lived in the back garden of a townhouse, and his owner had made the sentimental mistake of not having him castrated. He was no longer a cuddly pet but a very large and powerful black ram with an impressive set of horns, no respect for people, and brimming with testosterone. This monster rejoiced in the name of Willie, which may have suited him once but was far too benign for him now.

The phone call was a plea for help. Willie was standing on the back veranda and would not let his owner out of the house. This was serious, as the toilet door opened onto this verandah, and to reach it one had to come out of the back door and cross several feet of wooden planking. Willie had placed himself strategically to get anyone who tried this. He was standing in charge mode, making it quite clear what he was going to do with those formidable horns.

'I think this is a job for two strong men,' my husband told our eldest son, then in his mid-teens, and off they went on what they obviously felt was an amusing and fun mission. I wasn't so sure. Had I known what a monster, in every way, they would return with, I would have gone to any length to prevent them leaving home. Any hope I had that they would simply remove Willie from the verandah and allow access to the toilet was dashed when they returned with him. They put him in the nearest paddock to the house, a fairly small pleasant paddock with a dam. He should have gone in the farthest from the house, one without a dam. Truth was they decanted him as quickly as possible in the nearest place.

The move did not improve Willie. He seemed to see it as an upgrade, a larger area to lord it over, and more creatures, both two legged and four, to terrorise. We soon discovered he did not bluff. If you happened to be in the paddock and you saw him preparing to charge, you got out as quickly as you could; through the gate from choice, otherwise the fence, or failing that into the dam, but you did not stay in the paddock. My husband was brave enough and strong enough to stand his ground, catch him by those formidable horns, and throw him when he was the target.

Willie did not care for this, and after a couple of times left him alone. He was essentially a bully. The rest of us, animals and humans, were frankly terrified. We attempted to move him to a more distant location and co-opted Molly, our best and bravest stock horse, to help. Even she who had been known to stand her ground and turn the most unruly steers, decided discretion was definitely the better part of valour when she saw him going into the all too familiar precharge stance of lowered head. So he stayed where he was and most of us tried to avoid going in that paddock. When we had to, we chose a time when he was a good distance away and even then we only just made it to the gate in time. The sound of his head butting the gate and the sound of horn hitting iron behind you was a chilling one; you prayed the gate would hold.

Pepita lived mostly in this paddock. She liked it because it was in the centre of things and she could see what was going on. It did not present a problem to me because I only had to stand at the gate and call her and she came. Willie never came after her so it was easy to get her out. This in itself was strange. Careful observation revealed something even stranger. Willie treated Pepita with respect. Total respect. He sometimes forgot himself with my husband even though he knew how to deal with him. We all puzzled over this because Pepita was the gentlest, kindest, least aggressive of all our many equines, donkeys or ponies, and no one had ever seen her so much as threaten him.

Then one early Spring day—Pepita was still wearing her rug at night, but on sunny days I took it off for her—the animals in the paddock were all enjoying hay as the new grass was barely coming through. I saw that Willie was way off on the other side of the paddock, also eating hay, so I deemed it safe to go through the fence nearest to Pepita and remove her rug. I was on my way back to the fence carrying the rug when I looked behind me and saw Willie head down, with me in his sights. I eyed the fence and was pretty sure I wouldn't make it, hampered as I was by the heavy canvas rug. I looked back towards Pepita; I was definitely nearer her. If I could get back to her I was pretty sure he wouldn't touch me. I made a split second decision to get back and stand by her.

As I stumbled towards her as fast as I could with the rug in my arms, I called to her, more of a panic-stricken bleat than anything. I could see Willie coming—fast! 'Pepita—save me!' I had no real expectation of her doing anything but knew that if I stood close to her 'til he moved away or other help arrived, I would be safe.

She lifted her head from her hay and looked at me, then turned and saw Willie, and summed up the situation immediately—and acted. Her long ears flattened on her neck, her lips curled back, showing an impressive array of teeth, and she charged before he could.

Faced with a dose of his own medicine, Willie stopped dead in his tracks, then turned tail and ran—right to the other end of the paddock. Pepita followed far enough to make sure he really was going, and then turned and trotted back to me and her unfinished breakfast. I was awestruck. When she reached me she gave me not one but two firm nudges. I knew she was saying, 'Don't worry dear—I've dealt with him.' I put my arms round her neck, and with my face buried in her mane, breathed the dear familiar smell of her. In that moment our roles were reversed; she was the maternal one and I was the child as I mumbled, 'Thank you, thank you.'

She gave me another poke which I knew meant, 'Stop fussing and let me eat my breakfast.' I picked up the rug and left the paddock. I went inside, thankful that it was morning coffee time. As I regaled my husband with an account of my adventure, he seemed to accept it as the sort of thing Pepita might be expected to do. For my part, I felt both proud and humble, and we were both puzzled at how she had won Willie's respect.

I knew now that I had won Pepita's love as well as her confidence, but would I prove worthy? I was all too well aware that we humans so often failed to reach the same level of emotional commitment in our relationships with our animal friends as they did. We betrayed them time and again. I knew I had often been guilty, citing the need to be practical and not overly sentimental as the excuse when we failed them. I hoped the time would never come when I felt that way about Pepita and vowed to keep faith with her until death parted us.

Chapter Eighteen

How often I had lightly said, 'Living with a mule is like a good marriage—*'til death us do part.*' The experience with Willie had been a defining moment, convincing me that it was not just a nice sentimental idea that our affection for each other was mutual; it was also very real. This was the only time in our twenty-eight years together that Pepita ever came remotely near to deliberately hurting any other creature. She knew Willie's threat was real not mere posturing, and he for his part, had no illusions that she meant business.

Her response was totally unexpected; I had only hoped that he would not touch me if I were close enough to her side. My heartfelt, and rather pathetic, cry, 'Pepita—save me,' must have touched a protective chord in her, and indeed in that awful moment when I saw him preparing to charge and knew I had no hope of reaching safety, I did become almost an infant bleating for its mother. I thought about this incident a great deal and wondered why of all the creatures on the property, Pepita alone had instilled some respect into Willie? It remained an unsolved mystery.

Her early life spent on the tether proved useful. She had a tendency to founder, or to give the correct name to this painful affliction,

Laminitis. Good spring grass was the signal for this so we would put her on the tether, where she did an excellent job keeping the grass down in areas such as the drive. The coarse, dry grass here was far better for her than the lush green of spring paddocks. She was sensible and clever on a tether after so much early training and knew how to extricate herself from trouble. Better still, she seldom got it wound round her legs or any other obstacle. All the same, I never left her on it when we went out.

The story I heard when we were living in Tasmania of the young donkey who had been left alone on a tether and was attacked by a dog, causing it to panic and hang itself, remained in my memory.

She seemed to know when she needed to be tethered, and often got across to us that was where she wanted to be before we saw signs that she was treading carefully on tender feet. I do not know how she did this but in the same way that we knew in Autumn that she needed her rug on, we knew she should be on the tether.

She was an excellent judge of character, like so many animals. We, who judge people so much by outward trappings, are not nearly so adept at this. When she met a new person, she would treat them to a long hard stare; if they seemed as if they might be worth knowing, she walked up closer and extended her soft muzzle. People who passed this test could then stroke her. If closer inspection, on her part, didn't encourage her to want to know them, she stepped back a pace or so, her eyes would grow ever larger and rounder, and she would then look from them to me and back again. Sometimes she would even breathe heavily, not quite a snort. When this happened, and fortunately it was not too often, as she liked far more people than she disliked, I felt quite embarrassed and glad they did not seem to understand the message she was conveying to me. Over the years I learned to trust her judgment. I cannot remember an occasion when she made a mistake; I wish I could say the same about myself. I would have been spared the pain of trust bestowed unwisely had I taken notice of her in the first place.

I am glad to say these occasions were few and far between. The great majority of people she liked, some she even gave an A-plus, rating them very high on her personal *decent human being* scale. A few rare individuals she decided on first acquaintance were more than all right—they topped the scale. To these people she would offer the ultimate accolade: the invitation to scratch her rump. Reactions to this varied from being completely unnerved, seeing only the mule heels turned towards them, to puzzlement.

We had moved, and she had not yet met the local vet when he came to see a pony to whom he had to give an injection. With the syringe still in his hand he stopped to speak to Pepita in the next stable. She treated him to her usual scrutiny then swung round and backed up to him.

'What does she want?' he asked.

'She wants her bum scratching,' I told him, 'It means she likes you.'

'I like her too,' he replied. 'I will certainly oblige.' He added action to his words and gave her a vigorous scratching, just how she liked it, and just where she liked it, close to the top of her tail, which she moved to one side for him, screwing her head round to look at him. He still had the syringe in his hand, a fact he commented on as we turned away.

'I feel really flattered,' he told me. 'I had forgotten I still had this thing in my hand,' he indicated the syringe, 'and she still wanted me to scratch her.'

'You are quite right,' I told him. 'She has a hearty dislike of needles but she obviously knew you had no intention of jabbing it into her.'

She was correct, as always, in her assessment of him. I have known many excellent vets over the years but few who had such a genuine love and understanding of animals.

We had a Palomino mare at the time that cut her leg badly on the steel dropper of the fence when she was fooling about in the paddock. He came at the time and several times afterward to dress the wound. She always came straight up to the fence when he arrived, and even after she was entirely healed she would call out to him and come up when he came to see one of the other horses or donkeys. He was very touched by this and said that although he must have hurt her, she obviously knew that he was also helping her.

'Til death us do part. I still say it, only nowadays I mean it. And I am thinking of the 'old style' marriage, not the modern version, which is more like *'Til you don't please me any more.* I simply could not conceive of ever parting company with Pepita.

When I first had her I set out to educate her. I suppose to a certain extent I had achieved that goal, but over our years together, she had taught me far more. Her lessons had not been superficial ones however. She had taught me so much about the meaning of life and the oneness of all creation. I have always felt that the purpose of our existence here is primarily to learn. In the course of this learning we have to become the best we can of whatever we are. Now, I think it goes further that that; we need to help every living being whose paths intertwine with ours to become the best of whatever *they* are. Not appeal to the dark side of an animal's nature to encourage it to kill or hurt other creatures. If we do this we shall be held ultimately responsible.

I think, and hope, I may have done this with Pepita; given her the chance to become the best mule she could be. I hope so, and that in doing so I have lived up to the confidence her breeder had in me when she gave me the chance to buy her. I feel certain that through my relationship with Pepita I am a better person, or at least one with more appreciation of other souls, whatever type of body houses them.

Chapter Nineteen

As Pepita and I grew older, inevitably we also grew closer; just as two people who have lived together for many years tune into one another and can finish each other's sentences, so I felt I knew much of what she was thinking, and had no doubt that she was privy to my thoughts as well. This should not have surprised me, for the first time I ever heard an animal's voice loud and clear in my head, the message came from a horse, and in all probability, if I hadn't heard and acted on it, I would not be here today.

I have known and loved horses all my life. My father bred Shires, and I can remember the thrill of waking on Spring mornings to be told there was a new foal, and going out to the stable to inspect it. I have admired them for their strength and power, been awed by their control of it in deference to us feeble humans, loved many, feared a few, been overawed at times by their intelligence, and had my heart broken more than once. When I had my first donkey, and saw my first mule, my love extended to all equines, irrespective of the length of their ears.

Yet curiously enough, the horse that awoke in me an awareness of the many amazing qualities they possess, I only knew for a fraction of time. But it was such a powerful moment that it altered my view not only of all horses, but all animals in general.

I was in my teens at the time, and at a country horse show in England. My own little mare was resting between events, and I was watching the open horse jumping. As this was always a popular event, the spectators were two deep round the perimeter of the ring. One of the few exceptions was where I stood. A woman with a young child in a pusher was on my left, to my right there was a line of people against the rope, and another line behind. There was no one behind me, about the only spot where the line of spectators was just one person deep.

In came the next competitor, a rather thickset heavy man who was, I thought with youthful arrogance, an appalling rider. My sympathies were immediately with the horse. I had been taught to ride by Freda Newcombe;

she was well-known in English equestrian circles as the first woman to ride the length of the British Isles from Land's End to John O'Groats, but what I remember her for is her insistence that horses be treated with kindness and consideration at all times. She had many sayings to underline this: *Only one man in a hundred should wear spurs, and he should never use them,* was one. *There is no such thing as a cruel bit, only cruel hands,* another.

The only stick that should be carried by the rider was a hunting crop, she often said, explaining that the horn handle was useful to open gates, but it should never be used to hit the horse. I could almost hear her disapproval ringing in my head as I watched this contestant thundering around, whacking his poor horse with a stick. Quite unnecessarily, for it was willing and a good jumper. Then they came up to the wall, whack! whack! went the stick. I could see the horse was coming up to it wrong, he hadn't a hope of clearing it. He obviously knew this and ignored the sharp whack he got telling him to jump and stopped dead. The rider sailed over his head to land in a furious and undignified heap. The horse turned and made for the exit, no doubt relieved to be rid of the insensitive person on his back, and immediately this escape route from the arena was filled with more angry men, the official stewards, who waved their arms and shouted and threatened with more sticks. My heart surged with sympathy for the horse that turned back and galloped round the arena heading for the exit at the other end, only to be confronted by more men. It didn't seem to occur to anyone that the horse was now badly frightened and desperately looking for an escape. Here was proof that there was little rapport with his owner; a more kind and sympathetic person would have easily caught the horse.

As he galloped round he saw that the weakest spot was where I was standing. He changed direction and galloped straight at me. I could not move to the left because of the pusher, or to the right because of spectators in my way. The only place to go was backward, and that was where the horse would land if he jumped, and it looked as if that was what he intended. For what seemed an aeon yet must only have been a second, I found myself looking directly into his eyes, and in that brief moment, I heard a voice inside my head saying clearly, *'I'm going to jump. Duck!'*

Without hesitation I obeyed. I felt the rush of air as he went over me and heard the thud as he landed behind me. When I looked up he was gone, galloping in triumphant freedom about the showground, pursued of course by angry men with sticks. No one but me was aware of the small miracle that had occurred right in front of them; no one except my father, who had observed the incident from a short distance away.

'What made you duck?' he asked.

I answered with the simple truth. 'The horse told me to.'

'What a good job you understood—and obeyed,' was his reply in complete acceptance of my answer. 'That horse can jump all right—when he hasn't got a fool rider on his back giving him the wrong instructions,' he added.

I agreed and thought no more of it at the time, but over the years this incident has often recurred in my thoughts and had a profound influence on my thinking towards animals. When I have received a clear message from an animal and been tempted to ignore it and let my so-called logical mind take over, I have remembered the horse whose dramatic message probably saved my life. I realised that the horse had cared about me, a mere human who he didn't even know, and that what I had seen in his eyes that day was evidence that he was much more than flesh, blood and bone; there was something else there. This was probably the first time I knew without doubt that animals, like ourselves, were spirits, temporarily housed within a body.

This truth was confirmed whenever I looked into Pepita's large and beautiful eyes so full of expression, what one friend always referred to as her *speaking eyes*. I knew it as surely as I did when I looked into the eyes of my dog.

This flow of communication between us was

very real. I knew when she felt it was time to have her rug on in autumn, when her feet were getting tender in Spring, and she knew when I wanted to ride her, and when I was on her she knew when I wanted to turn left, or right or which direction I wanted to go—not that she always agreed, far from it.

How was it then that I failed to get the message when she was telling me so clearly about the tree about to fall? It must have been both frustrating and alarming for her. Not only was I too dense to understand, but I had actually tied her up in the danger spot. When the tree split in half and came crashing down next day in the exact place where she had been standing, I received the message she transmitted to me very clearly indeed.

I ran across the space between us and scrambled through the fence to her side, where I flung my arms round her neck and buried my face in her sweet smelling mane. I was overcome with emotion then. I could have lost her, and it would have been entirely my own fault. Just because I was so taken up in the practical business of the day, I had no time to listen to her. It was as if I had switched off the communication channel between us as casually as I would the radio. It was no excuse, especially as my attention had been drawn to the fact that there was something wrong when she refused the biscuits a kind friend had brought especially for her.

'I'm so sorry,' I mumbled into her neck. 'Can you ever forgive me?'

She nudged me somewhat vigorously, and I knew that she had.

Chapter Twenty

As the years passed and Pepita entered the last years of her life, I only rode her in the paddock where she lived. She was always delighted when I produced her saddle and bridle, and appeared to enjoy herself as much as I did.

I still had her pedestal and she was still eager to go up on it, but it now had another use. I used it as a mounting block to get myself up into the saddle. Even though she was small, I found it difficult to summon the spring necessary to get up into the saddle. But the pedestal was small, not like the large stone mounting block at the gateway of my childhood home in England.

This relic of the days when real horsepower was the standard means of transport had always been there, part of the environment, and I found it invaluable when I wanted to ride my spotted mare bareback. This kind and gentle pony had a thing about people vaulting on her bareback; she simply would not allow it. She had no objections to being ridden without the saddle, provided the rider lowered themselves carefully onto her back and didn't try any clever gymnastics.

I had never been blessed with a great deal of *spring,* unlike my husband, who when demonstrating to the children how to vault onto a horse had so much, he landed on the ground on the other side, to the delight of his audience. Even though I loved to ride Pepita, getting on was a problem as advancing years and stiffening joints robbed me of what little spring I had, so I used her pedestal.

The snag was that it had to be in just the right place for me to land in the saddle and not on her neck or rump. I would move it to get it just right, and then she moved a step backward, forward or sideways, and it was not in the correct place at all. So I decided to ask her, very politely of course, for her assistance.

Even though I had confidence that she would understand the problem and my need for her co-operation, I was still amazed how quickly she grasped what I needed her to do. I reversed the order, and instead of moving the pedestal to where I wanted it, I first put it in approximately the right place, then stood on it and gave her verbal instructions just as if she were a human being. 'A step forward, (or back),' I told her. Or 'A bit closer, (or not so close).' She knew exactly what I wanted her to do and I was able to mount her as quickly as I had ever done. Her willingness to help me in this way convinced me that she enjoyed our sedate ambles around the paddock every bit as much as I did.

Pepita had always had a sense of fun. There are those that deny animals have a sense of humour, but no one can really say that they do not enjoy a game and even a joke. All of which adds up to a sense of fun, at least. Most dogs and cats retain their willingness to enjoy a game well into their mature, even older years. This is one of the reasons we like their company; they help to preserve our own youth. They are not alone in this. Equines, indeed, most happy, healthy animals love a game. Horses laugh when they are playing together in the paddock by high tailing it; they gallop round with their tails stuck up at an absurd angle. Donkeys show their enjoyment by dashing around with their nose stuck in the air. Pepita went to the donkey side of her ancestry when she was in a frivolous mood.

I had found her humour embarrassing and infuriating at times when she chose to act dumb and pretend she did not know what I was asking her to do, but I did not deny its existence. I once had a Jersey house cow that taught me that a cow could have a sense of humour when she thought up a joke of which I was the victim.

The stall where I milked May had a wooden lever which when lifted opened the door in front of her to let her out after milking. She knew how this worked as well as I did, and I

104

had to tie this bar with hay band so that she could not push it up to keep her there until the job was finished. The morning routine was that I put her breakfast in the trough, she walked into the stall and I secured the lever with hay band, placed the bucket and stool in position and milked her while she ate her breakfast. If I forgot to tie the lever, May waited 'til I sat down on the stool, then knocked the lever up with her horn and walked out, leaving me sitting on a milking stool with a bucket in front of me but no cow to milk. She invariably walked around the yard and back into her stall to eat the breakfast she had abandoned in order to enjoy her joke. If a cow can have a twinkle in her eye she definitely did, and I was only too well aware that I must have looked very foolish all set to milk a cow that wasn't there. Having been the butt of this joke of May's more times than I like to remember, I never doubted Pepita's sense of humour.

She was good friends with my dog, a lovable and intelligent Labrador/Kelpie cross. Ashley liked to go through the wire fence into our neighbour's paddock. If my daughter happened to be with me she came back immediately for her because she knew that if she didn't, Ruth would climb over the fence and get her back. She knew equally well that I wouldn't, or couldn't. She greatly over-estimated Pepita's ability however, and firmly believed she was capable of getting through, or over, the fence with me on her back.

I took advantage of this mistaken belief, and when I was riding Pepita and Ashley went through the fence, rode up to it and told her to come back. She always obeyed when I was on Pepita, just as she always ignored me when I was on my own two feet. After I had done this a couple of times, Pepita understood and I only had to say to her, 'Come on—get her back!' and she dashed up to the fence and Ashley scrambled back as fast as her own elderly and portly body allowed, tongue lolling in a sheepish grin and tail wagging as she did so

Even though we were not going anywhere, just pottering in the paddock, Pepita still liked to argue with me about the direction we would take. Up came her hind foot in the direction of my heel. The feeling of a corkscrew under the saddle was familiar to me, as this was her way of expressing disapproval of the direction I wanted to go. Over the many years I had ridden her, she had done this at least once on every ride, yet her hoof and my heel had never connected. Our combined ages had reached the century before it ever did, but it did not hurt in the least, I just felt a tap on the heel of my boot accompanied by the sound of hoof hitting leather. Pepita was far more fazed than I was. She put her foot down on the ground and stood stock still for a moment, before going in the direction of my choice. She was, apparently, shocked by her success, for she never did it again. That was the one and only time her foot ever connected with mine. It had never worried me; I always knew there was no intent to hurt in it, it was just one of her many ways of communicating with me, as familiar and free of malice as her nudges.

*   *   *

Sadly, our riding days were drawing to a close. There was a special magic in the company of my little mule, my friend and companion for twenty-eight years. We were as close, or closer than ever. The species barrier disappeared and we were just two elderly ladies enjoying our retirement and the company of the other. I remembered more active and exciting times together as we ambled in a leisurely manner around the paddock. I wondered if Pepita's thoughts were running along the same lines.

I found these quiet rides as reviving and relaxing as a deep meditation. Just pottering about the paddock on Pepita's back gave me some of the happiest times I ever enjoyed in the saddle. The feeling of companionship between us was as strong, or stronger than it had ever been. I wished these pleasant peaceful days could last forever. A useless wish, for nothing does. That one of us had four legs and the other only two was neither here nor there. The knowledge and understanding of each other, including our weaknesses and foibles, that had developed over the years had its own soothing magic.

The last time I rode her our combined ages were a hundred, something of a record in itself. We might have made it more if events had not forced me to move yet again. But we were not parted; I managed to lease a vacant block for her next to the suburban house I moved to when circumstances forced me to sell the rural property where we had lived happily in retirement for the last five years.

Chapter Twenty-One

Pepita accepted the change in our circumstances, just as she had always done with all our moves, and settled without any trouble. There had been one period when we had to live in separate places. I was never tempted to sell her any more than I would consider selling a member of my family. Correction, my *human* family. She was a member of the family.

For a period we lived in a townhouse without a convenient vacant block next door. When we moved there it was only intended to be temporary, but it turned out to be several years. Pepita went to live on my daughter's property and I visited her and went out and rode her when I could. I missed having her so close. In the last home we shared together I could go out at any time of the day and talk to her over the garden fence. I didn't ride her after this last move. A building block in the middle of houses is not exactly good riding country.

Mules are one of the marvels of nature, bred from a horse mother and a donkey father, they should not, in theory, exist, as donkeys and horses have a different number of chromosomes, but they do and are bred in great numbers in many parts of the world. Anyone who has ever known and loved a mule will tell you they have a magic unique to themselves. Combining in one animal the special qualities of both horses and donkeys, they are extremely intelligent, with remarkable memories and capable of great devotion to those lucky enough to win it. On the other hand, they will not forget abuse or ill treatment, and may wait for years to get their own back on the offender.

I was once told by a veteran of the Burma campaign in World War Two who had worked with both elephants and mules, that the former were incredible animals. Everything one heard about them was true, but every now and then he had cause to wonder if mules did not have the edge on them.

One thing all mule people seem to agree on was that training a mule is not a job for the fainthearted. Maybe I didn't do such a bad job after all.

The mule has been described as, *'Without pride of ancestry or hope of posterity,'* and this is how he is often looked upon today. One of the most racist comments I ever heard was made to me apropos mules. It shocked me into speechlessness. I was talking to a horseman who I knew also liked donkeys, so I assumed he would be partial to mules. How wrong I was. When I asked how he liked my mule he replied, 'Put it this way; I feel the same about you having a mule as I would if my daughter came home with a black man.'

I stared at him; surely he must have been joking? But no, he was deadly serious. Was this the thinking of the Sydney Hunt Club when they refused to allow Juanita to join them? Fortunately the Endurance Riding people thought differently. After she had become the first mule to complete the prestigious Quilty, a visiting American endurance rider requested the privilege of having her as a mount when she took part in a ride in Australia.

Mules were not always thought of in this derogatory way. In Biblical times donkeys were for the people, horses for army officers, and mules for royalty. I cannot help but wonder if this did not stem from the innate mule character; mules have a reputation for looking after number one, and they would probably not be so willing to gallop wildly into battle as horses.

In Roman times, Nero's wife bathed in asses milk for her complexion, and had her mules shod with gold. Well into the Middle Ages they were carefully bred and highly prized in Europe. Cardinal Wolseley had two black mules that wore coverings of scarlet and cloth of gold to pull his carriage

This *care for themselves* instinct also means care for their rider. In more recent times, mules and hinnies were bred in large numbers as reliable and safe mounts for women and children, and I was told that as late as the nineteen twenties and thirties when the only way to get goods into parts of Queensland was by pack horse and mule, that eggs, china and young children were packed on the mules because they could be trusted not to knock their packs on trees or protruding rocks.

With the arrival in America of large mule breeding jacks from Spain following the initial gift of one, appropriately named Royal Gift, from the King of Spain to George Washington, they became an important part of the American economy; a valuable source of power, particularly on the Southern plantations. Mules were used extensively in Agriculture up to the beginning of World War Two. Large teams were also used in the trek west to open up the country.

Today, these working mules have been largely replaced by lighter animals, and are popular in all forms of pleasure riding and to carry tourists down the Grand Canyon where their good sense and surefootedness are appreciated.

In 1980, Joshua A. Lee wrote a wonderful book called *With Their Ears Pricked Forward— Tales of Mules I Have Known*. At the time of writing the book he was Professor of Crop Science at North Carolina State University, but he had been brought up on a plantation in Georgia and remembered the time when mules were a vital part of agriculture. In those days, he tells us, *'being a good judge of mules was important enough to be recorded in a man's epitaph.'* The stories in this book, however incredible, are entirely believable to anyone like me who lived with a mule for twenty-eight years and had passing acquaintance with other mules along the way.

Until she died at almost thirty-two, I found a special magic in the company of my little mule. To me, she was always beautiful, even when grey hairs peppered her head and her figure was not the best. After all, the same had happened to me. Best of all were her eyes, always so full of expression.

We shared a loving friendship for over a quarter of a century. Pepita was more than an exceptional mule, she was an exceptional soul.

Chapter Twenty-Two

One of the hardest things I ever had to do in my whole life was agree with the advice of the vet I had called in when Pepita, who had never known a day's illness in her life, was obviously in pain when I saw her first thing on that fateful Spring morning.

She appeared to have colic, which is a severe complaint in all equines, and dreaded by their owners. I do not know whether mules are susceptible to it in their old age but I have known it be the cause of death of more than one mule.

The vet instructed me to keep her moving, so I did my best to comply, but when she kept throwing herself on the ground and her eyes which hitherto had looked to me to make things better clouded over as if she could not focus on me, and it became almost impossible to keep her on her feet, let alone walking, I was forced to agree with the young woman vet I had called that the kindest thing was a lethal injection.

I knew she was right and that I had to do this last act of love for my darling friend. I could not bury her in a suburban garden or in a rented block, nor did I want to. My daughter, who was with us when she died, generously offered to have her buried on her property, so my son and son-in-law attended to that. I was so grateful to them all. I felt as if I had lost a piece of myself and was not able to think cohesively.

I wrote an obituary notice which was published in many of the animal and equine journals I wrote for, and I received a lot of sympathy. One in particular not only touched me, but also filled me with gratitude. Pam Adams, who is a well-known animal communicator and author of the book *Angels Who Came With Fur and Four Paws,* is also a civil celebrant, and she offered to conduct a service in Pepita's memory, as a gift.

This was held in the paddock where she was buried.

Another friend, who runs a cremation service for dogs and cats, had the brilliant idea of bringing a basket full of pieces of carrot and apple, which she scattered on the ground, and this brought up Pepita's many equine friends to join us.

Pam conducted a beautiful little ceremony, which far from being sad, was a celebration of Pepita's long and wonderful life. The eulogy I had written for her was read, and the little service ended with a reading of the poem I wrote on her death. We then went into the house for afternoon tea.

This ceremony was a truly wonderful gift. It was not only a celebration of her life but also helped to bring closure, or so I thought, but it

114

was not the end.

I have another friend in Hobart, Leonora Faferko who is a spiritual clairvoyant, and author of the book *Heartspeak*. She specialises in receiving messages from beloved animals who have passed on, and when she heard Pepita was dead, she asked me to email a photo of her so she could try to contact her. In her reply to me, she missed off the a on Pepita, telling me this was not a typing error but was the pet name I had used for her. When she contacted Pepita's spirit, she had communicated that she had always liked it better than her real name. This was entirely true, and something Leonora could not have known. When we were alone and no one could hear me I always dropped the final syllable and called her *Pippit,* but more often, *my darling Pippit.*

When I read this, I felt sure she was indeed waiting for me, as I had asked her to do in the poem I wrote straight from my heart just after she died. She had also communicated to Leonora that she had enjoyed the ceremony after her death, as it had made her feel that she was not *just a thing.*

Indeed she was not.

More Than a Mule

(For Pepita. 25/11/1970—05/10/2002)
Just a mule—my head tells me,
And your photo confirms
That you indeed had long ears,
A tail and four hooves.
But I remember your eyes
And the friendship we shared.
You were not 'Just' anything.
Your intelligence, humour, and
Big, loving heart
Added up to a special soul;
An eternal Spirit who, God willing,
Has found green pasture,
Shady trees and old friends.
Enjoy— 'til I come looking for you.

278

sq 6

2

60

720